THE JOY OF OLD

Grow in joy

This book is dedicated to the many elders
who opened for us the geode of age
and revealed to us the marks of successful elders.

THE JOY OF OLD

A Guide to Successful Elderhood

John S. Murphy
and
Frederic M. Hudson

Geode Press
Altadena, California

ISBN 1-886851-44-1
Library of Congress Catalog Card Number 95-094012

Geode Press
P.O. Box 6077
Altadena, CA 91003-6077

Illustrations and book design by John S. Murphy
Cover by Nanette Boyer Design

Printed in the United States of America

Cataloging Data
Murphy, John S.
    The joy of old: a guide to successful elderhood /
John S. Murphy and Frederic M. Hudson
    160 p. : ill. ; 23cm.
    Includes index.
    ISBN 1-886851-44-1
    1. Aged—Life skills guides. 2. Aged—Psychology.
    1. Hudson, Frederic M.
    646.79—dc20   95-094012

Contents

About the Authors

John S. Murphy, PhD, is a psychotherapist, speaker, and author. A WWII veteran and a computer pioneer since 1950, he wrote several technical books from the introductory to the professional level, and was a partner in a small entrepreneurial firm. In mid-career, he earned a doctorate in psychology at age 53. Married over 44 years, he has six children and ten grandchildren. He is director of Elder Seminars at The Hudson Institute of Santa Barbara.

Frederic M. Hudson, PhD, is a consultant, writer, speaker, and scholar in adult development and renewal. He was the founding president of Fielding Institute, a leading and innovative professional graduate school for adults. In 1987 he founded The Hudson Institute of Santa Barbara to train adults in the mastery of life change. His other books include *The Adult Years: Mastering the Art of Self-Renewal* (Jossey-Bass, 1991) and *LifeLaunch: A Passionate Guide to the Rest of Your Life* (with Pamela D. McLean, Hudson Institute Press, 1994)

Both authors, dissatisfied with the popular prospect of aging, used the work of creating this book to find a more positive foundation for our own elderhood, and to embrace our age more fully.

Acknowledgments

We are grateful for all the help we got along the way. Our helpers include those who shared their experience and ideas at seminars and workshops over the last several years. They include those who encouraged us and gave guidance and criticism as our work evolved. And they include those elders whose lives and example quietly revealed to us the secrets of successful elderhood.

Among the many, we are especially grateful to Ron Aday, Peggy Azad, Clare Corbett, Marion Davis, Francesca di Franco, Joe Dillon, Mary Dreyer, Elizabeth Dorsey, Barbara Gaughen, Fontelle Gilbert, Sandra Goudy-Andrew, Richard Haid, Gary Hammond, Wendy Helms, Joan Minninger, Robert Manley, Don and Traute Moore, Marilyn Rampley, Tobe Reisel, Nicole Rhodes, Dean Shetler, Lucy Scott, Sally Stewart, and Carol Terry. For her pervasive influence, special gratitude is due to that great teacher and family therapist, Virginia Satir.

Foreword

Many books are written about the troubles of the elderly; few about their advantages and challenges for growth and development. Little is written about healthy, vital, exemplary elders who want to live—as they have most of their lives—with dreams, plans, and promises to keep. This book is for them.

In the early years of this century, the notion of "retirement" was invented to remove older workers from the labor market, so that younger workers could advance and prosper. By 1960 or so our whole culture was treating retirement as a natural, predictable, and desirable thing. A large "retirement market" of activities and communities designed for people over sixty now promotes and provides retirement living on the margins of main stream living. A national association for these people, the American Association of Retired People (AARP) quickly evolved to become the largest lobby in Washington—for retired people, not fully-engaged people who attain a certain age.

Yet retirement as we know it is not a natural part of human development. The notion sprang from the needs of labor and industry, not from adult developmentalists. Retirement means, literally, to draw back from the world of work. It is a disengagement from our careers and full incomes, often involving a separation from friends, organizations, and sense of purpose.

The retirement market promotes financial security as the most important consideration, with leisure activity as the second. While both of these are very important for elder development, neither produces human fulfillment without being part of a larger scheme that includes new dreams, work of some sort, human connections, and meaning.

We grow older in a culture that does not expect much from us as elders, other than predictable decline and medical needs. We elders are not challenged to grow and become more; we are expected to fade and become less. There are few positive roles for elders, as leaders, workers, or mentors. We seldom reward elders with demanding assignments—the Jimmy Carters of the world must find them for themselves. We encourage elders to retire to fun city where they can be outside the main culture, and behave as predictable consumers in a niche market. The greatest resource our society squanders is the talent, developed or latent, of those over sixty.

The natural evolution of adult life is to **protire**—to modify work commitments but to stay engaged in the total flow of life. *Elderhood is a time in life for each of us to gain our highest level of consciousness, conscience, and mission as human beings. If we stay on course with the lives we have built and are still building, we create a value-added chapter that contributes to the culture, promoting candor and integrity.* We speak the truth as we see it. We laugh more and we have less to lose than ever before by being candid and clear.

Leisure becomes a vehicle for spiritual meaning, but so do work, family, and friends. Elders are naturally spiritual, because their bodies no longer define who they are. Their essence is fundamentally spiritual, expressed through beliefs, values, caring, and humor. The reservoir of elder experience finds a deep voice within that does not depend on the strength of body or the quality of speech. We are free to be, to do, and to love, as never before.

With advances in medicine and disease control, coupled with increased awareness of nutrition and exercise, adults are living longer. By the year 2000 there will be 100,000 Americans who have lived 100 years. Throughout the land there will be millions more elders who are healthy, talented, and eager to make a difference. Our culture provides little script for engaging this enormous human resource. We elders must invent new roles, traditions, and rituals for ourselves if we want to change the behavior of *old* in our country. We must find ways to embrace the future with expectancy and wonder. The call of the future determines the conscious activity of today, and elders who are "protiring" will draw themselves ahead with purpose and meaning.

A great awakening is about to happen in America and in all the major industrialized countries. It is a grey awakening with a loud voice, an income base, technical and human skills, fairly good health, and a determination to transform the social reality of *old*.

This book is a trumpet for this awakening, promoting developmental challenges for elders, evoking new leadership, and finding new paths for extraordinary persons with wrinkled bodies. If you read this book, a page at a time, and reflect on how the theme of each page relates to your growth as an elder, you will feel the challenge to stay vital and awake to the best years ahead of you.

—*Frederic M. Hudson*

Life calls for full living. Elder life calls for fuller living than ever before, but of a different sort. We fail if we withdraw from life, and we may also fail if we simply cling to an old style of life that no longer fits for us. We succeed when we keep adapting to change and reengaging vitally, according to who we are at this time, and what we value now.

Throughout life, we grow by passing through a series of experiments and transitions, reinventing and perfecting ourselves as we age. It should come as no surprise that we must invent our own elderhood as we approach it. There are no fixed specifications. This book is a guide to the trail, and a report about successful elders—those who have settled in the rich land of Elderhood and love living there.

We elders may be the quiet leaders in building a better world, not because we take positions of authority, but because we express, in our own lives, the human values that our society is seeking. Because we find the joy of *old*, and it is contagious.

May you find that joy in your own elderhood, and spread it widely.

—*John S. Murphy*

How to Use This Book

Each chapter is organized like a string of pearls. Each page is one of the pearls, covering a separate, simple topic, and supported by one or more illustrations so it is easy to grasp. Each page can be read as a separate unit. Although there is a gradual progression and development, one can easily browse amongst pages.

The book is addressed personally to you, the reader, so you are invited to consider the personal implications of each page. Each page ends with a question addressed to you, to personalize the meaning of the topic. You can find your reflection in each pearl if you look for it.

This book is *for* elders, not *about* them. It promotes the fullness of life and living in age. It advocates purpose, dignity, meaning, and joy for elders.

We elders are highly experienced people, so we ask, "How does this idea compare with my own experience?" We personalize what we read. And we are very practical, so we ask, "So what? How does it impact me? Is there anything I need to do about it?"

Most books are monologues, but elder readers prefer dialogue. This book presents short and simple ideas, and then invites your personal consideration and response.

We suggest you write down your responses to each page. Then your participation will be clearer and more effective for you. If you are reading your own copy of the book, you might like to write your responses in the margins. A better technique is to write them in a personal journal or separate notebook as you read. Or discuss the topics with your mate, a friend, or a group that is reading the book.

Play with the ideas, criticize them, personalize them, enjoy them, and embrace those that fit for you.

Although elderhood is not a definite age range, we address the book to readers sixty or older. If younger people read it—as they may, for it says some things about aging that may be of interest—we suggest they read it as if over the shoulders of elders, as welcome voyeurs.

Part I
How Do You Feel About Aging?

Most Americans approach age with bias, blindness, and fear. We are biased because we know the defects of age but not its positive qualities. We are blind because the richness, wisdom, peace, freedom, humor, and spirit of age are not well known— they are hidden from us until we discover them personally. We fear the loss, illness, weakness, isolation, and physical decline of age—these threats are well known. We see the dark side of aging but not its bright side, and we forget the dark side of being young.

It could be otherwise; other cultures appreciate and honor age. Even though we have forgotten the positive aspects of age, we can rediscover them. This book aims to help do so.

The time has come to find again the joy of old. There are more of us oldsters now than ever before. We are living longer, and need to be inspired by better ideas of how to be healthy, successful, and valuable. We need to rediscover and reinvent elderhood.

Chapter 1
Attitudes

First, we invite you to consider your attitudes toward your own aging, and to compare your views of aging, both positive and negative, with those of others.

Topics:

Questions About Aging

Familiar Refrains of Elderhood

Hidden Elderhood

Positive and Negative Views

The Rock of Age

Questions About Aging

Here are some important questions that you face as you age:

1. *Ordeal or Adventure?* For you, is growing older a trial or a welcome experience? Is it something you look forward to or something you dread?

2. *Expectation or Surprise?* Has your actual aging experience been better than or worse than you expected?

3. *Decline or Growth?* Are there parts of you that are growing, emerging, or improving as you get older? Or is aging only a downhill decline?

4. *Continuation or Change?* So far, are your older years a simple continuation of your earlier life, or is there a major change in your philosophy and attitudes, in what you value and hold most important, and in how you live and spend your energy from day to day?

5. *Homogenous or Diverse?* Do you find older people all alike or remarkably different, predictably common or surprisingly diverse?

6. *Death-dominated or Life-centered?* How do you deal with the realization that death is getting closer? How does this issue, and the way you cope with it, affect the quality of your life?

7. *Joyless or Joyful?* Is there joy in your elderhood? Our culture suggests there is not much available. Some find there is a lot.

POSITIVE? NEGATIVE?

HOPE? DESPAIR?

Where do you stand on these seven issues? Write out your first thoughts, then read on to discover both the popular answers to these questions and new ideas for choosing your own more joyous path ahead.

Familiar Refrains of Elderhood

When we ask people of any age their thoughts and feelings about growing old, here are some of the most common themes we hear:

"I want to stay young as long as I can."

"I want to have enough money."

"I don't want to be physically or financially dependent on anyone, not even my children."

"I may be lonely."

"I don't want to be bored and out of touch, so I'm going to keep working as long as I can."

"I want to have more fun, and travel more."

"I have a long list of things I haven't yet had time for."

"I may lose my health."

"I don't want to be a vegetable."

Money, recreation, intimacy, health—these issues and others are prominent for most people when they think about aging.

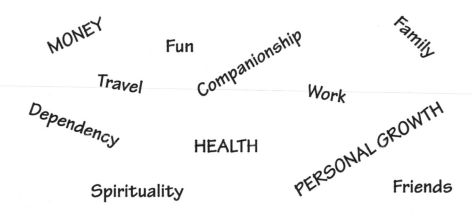

. . . .

As you contemplate your aging, what hopes or fears are most prominent for you? Record your list of hopes and fears.

Hidden Elderhood

Here are some other views that are heard from people who are already into their elderhood and have discovered by experience some of its qualities:

"Overall, I am more comfortable with the world around me now."

"I want to keep on growing and maturing."

"I'm freer than I ever was before."

"I want to be of service, to make a difference."

"I feel out of the mainstream, yet I'm finally doing things that are really important to me."

"I appreciate people and things much more than I used to."

"I suppose I understand more than when I was younger, but more important, I have more respect for what I don't understand."

"My life is more balanced now."

"I feel very grateful."

This is a part of elderhood that is not well known. Elders do not often speak of these things, perhaps because they are not expected to or asked to. If you do ask, you must enter into dialogue and listen carefully to discover what they mean. Out of such dialogue there emerges a picture of the Hidden Elderhood— what some elders discover through the actual experience of growing older. It is in this hidden part of elderhood that the joy of old is found.

Freedom Appreciation Maturity Service Balance Gratitude

. . . .

Which of these are important to your life at this time? What else would you add?

Positive and Negative Views

To clarify your own views on elderhood, try the following exercise:

Jot down on a page of your notebook, as quickly as they come to your mind, a few adjectives or nouns that seem to you to describe older people. Then divide the page into two columns, labeled Negative and Positive. Sort the words you have generated into these two categories. Which column is longest and strongest?

We sometimes ask groups to give us a few words describing elderhood as they see it, then classify their responses as positive or negative. Here is a sampling of the typical result:

NEGATIVE	POSITIVE
Feeble	Wise
Jaded	Experienced
Worthless	Passionate
Finished	Interesting
Dull	Vital
Sexless	Valuable
Rigid	Mature
Sick	Loving

The negative descriptions are more likely to come from younger people; the positive ones, from older people. Younger people often do not understand the positive responses, or discount them as rationalization.

The negative view generally reflects our cultural attitude toward aging. We discover the positive view as we actually experience age.

. . . .

How can you promote conscious aging, emphasizing its positive features, in your life?

The Rock of Age

Elderhood is like a geode, a special kind of stone. From the outside a geode looks like a coarse and ordinary rock. Hidden inside is a cluster of beautiful, crystalline gems. Like a geode, elderhood is crusty, weathered, and earthy on the outside; it is beautiful, sparkling, rich and mysterious on the inside.

As we first approach elderhood, we see only the outside surface—we see an ordinary rock that is rough, tarnished, encrusted with earthy history. It gives little hint of the treasure within.

Our youth-centered culture, seeing the surface of this rock of age, judges it unattractive and without value. It has not yet discovered the core of age. As we grow old, our culture sees us as weathered and of little worth, unaware that we contain a treasure. We have the choice of living with this outer appearance or searching for the treasure within. To reveal the treasure we must cut through the encrusted old assumptions that cover up the gems within us. In this book we cut open the geode of elderhood, look within, polish it up a bit, and reveal the beauty of age.

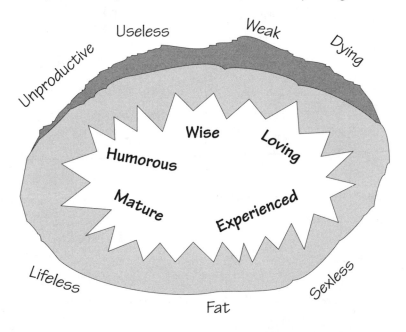

Consider yourself a geode. What do you see on the inside? On the outside? What do you think others see?

Chapter 2

Three Threads of Aging

Three interwoven threads run throughout the fabric of life, and strongly influence our attitudes about aging.

Topics:

The Threads

The Three Peaks of Life

Weaving the Threads Together

The Path Through Life

The Three Vehicles of Life

The Three Biases of Life

Base, Support, and Essence

Decline and Emergence in Elderhood

The Threads

It is most useful to consider aging in terms of three themes that run like threads throughout life. They are:

♦ *The Physical Thread.* The condition of our bodies from birth to death.

♦ *The Economic Thread.* The condition of our material and monetary wealth throughout life.

♦ *The Human Thread.* Our condition as a developing and maturing person from birth to death.

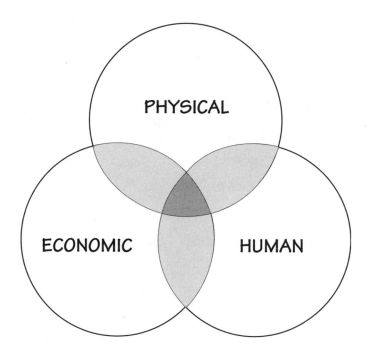

These are dynamic themes, and we weave them together into the tapestry of our elder years. Following the human thread, our bodies grow and change. Following the economic thread, we become productive and support ourselves and others. Following the human thread, we blossom and mature as persons.

. . . .

How do you weave together these three threads? How do all three work together in positive ways?

The Three Peaks of Life

Physical energy tends to grow until it reaches a peak relatively early in life; thereafter it slowly and gradually declines with age. Put simply, the popular physical view of life looks like this:

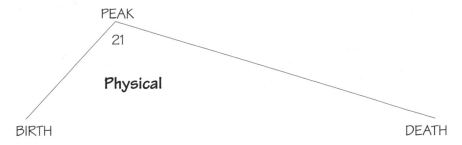

The economic view measures our productive capability and sees life in terms of "making a living." In the popular view it peaks at about age 40.

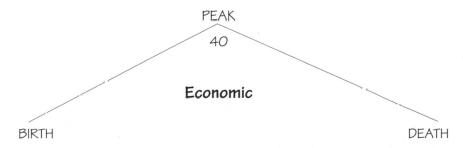

The human view measures our emergence as full persons. Personal development goes on throughout life. We keep on growing, and reach our "peak" only at death.

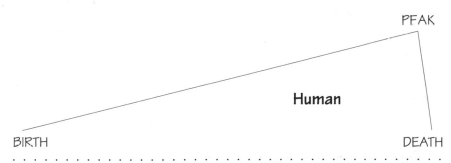

Looking backward and forward in your life, at what ages do you place your own physical, economic, and human peaks?

Weaving the Threads Together

No single thread provides an adequate view of aging, but woven together they provide a balanced view. Each thread adds its strength to the fabric of life. Each comes to the fore in its turn.

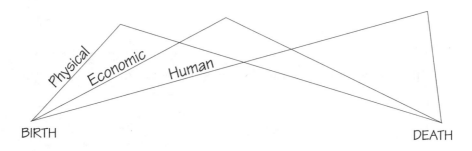

As seen over a lifetime, each of the threads is dominant at a different period. There are three peaks, which can be called the *salient* peaks of life. One of the meanings of the word "salient" is standing out, like a mountain peak. These are salient aspects of life in that they stand out above others.

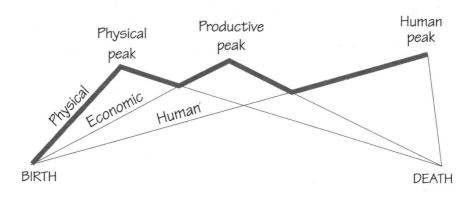

. . . .

Trace the three threads through your life. Are all three present now? Which is emerging? What is your growing edge? Be as specific as you can.

The Path Through Life

We go over these peaks in sequence. Life is a long trek through the mountains of our changing experience, in which we climb each of the salient peaks in turn. As we clear one peak, the next comes into view. For each peak, the climbing is different. The physical peak is steep and strenuous; the productive peak, long and plodding; the human peak, gentle but challenging

A typical path through life is a progressive transition from the physical peak to the productive peak to the human peak. This corresponds to three main phases of life: youth, midlife, and elderhood. Youth is the phase of life in which physical energy dominates, and the physical aspect of life is salient. Midlife is the phase in which productive energy dominates, and the economic aspect is salient. *Elderhood is the phase in which human energy dominates, and the human aspect of life is salient.*

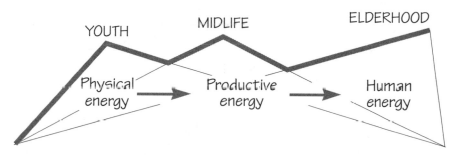

For a successful life, we must "climb every mountain," as the song from *Sound of Music* puts it. If we climb only the physical peak, we are too soon "over the hill," and most of life is decline. If we climb also the productive peak, still about half of life is in decline. If we climb also the human peak, there is always growth to offset decline, and we are never "over the hill."

The first two peaks are well known, the third is not. It may be hidden from view, and we may not discover it until late in our journey.

. . . .

What was your experience in moving from the physical to the productive peak? How are you now experiencing the shift from productive to human energy? How are you changing for the better?

The Three Vehicles of Life

A "vehicle" is that aspect of our lives that we rely upon to deliver our success and to carry our meaning. We build our lives on our perceived strength. Our youthful years are body-centered—our *body* is the vehicle by which we move on in life. It carries us along as a wave carries a surfboard. When we feel the youthful aliveness of our body, we have self-evident reason to believe in all of life. Our body seems to give us purpose and permanence. We catch the physical wave and ride it. We play, and take on roles of lover and sports activist.

In midlife we pursue money and productivity—our *work* becomes the vehicle of life. Our work gives us value and our acquisitions seem to give us a kind of permanence. We catch the economic wave and ride it. We work, save, graduate our children from school and from our homes, and move into leading roles in our communities.

In elderhood neither our body nor our work can remain the vehicle. We must find something inside us to take over and carry us through life. We search for our essence, and we find it. In maturity, our *self* is the vehicle of life.

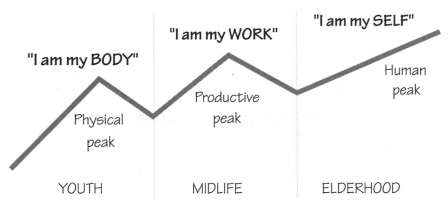

We need all three vehicles. Riding through life on one's body is not a mistake; it is what youth does naturally and well. Riding through life on ones work is what midlife does naturally and well. These vehicles gradually carry us on to the third vehicle, the self.

· ·

On your human journey, in what ways are you finding your "self," and how does it make you more alive?

The Three Biases of Life

Although all three facets are important, each phase of life has its special bias—it favors one aspect over the others.

In youth our energy goes primarily into *physical activity*, and the other two aspects are secondary. The physical aspect is at the center of life. This is the normal bias of youth.

In midlife our energy goes primarily into *productive activity* like earning a living, raising a family, building a career, and educating children. The other two aspects are, in comparison, secondary. This is the normal bias of midlife.

In elderhood it is natural for our energy to turn primarily to *core human issues* such as being in good relationship with ourselves and our mates, families, and friends. We gravitate toward the human essentials, build our lives around them, and live in that context as fully as we can. The physical and economic aspects, although important, are no longer at the center of our lives; they are secondary. This is the normal bias of elderhood.

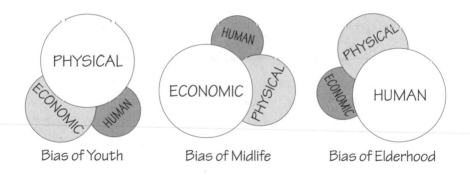

Bias of Youth   Bias of Midlife   Bias of Elderhood

In a broad sense, aging is a progressive journey through life, a gradual transition from physical emphasis to productive emphasis to human emphasis. Although our emphasis changes, at any age we need to consider all three aspects to achieve a balanced life.

· ·

What are your current commitments to physical activity, productive activity, and human issues in a typical week? Have you reached the bias of elderhood? Is it empowering or limiting?

Base, Support, and Essence

Each of the three aspects serves a different purpose.

The physical aspect is the *base* of life. It is the stuff that provides a body and a plan for its development. In itself the physical aspect provides no goal for life other than health and longevity.

The economic aspect is *support* for the process of living. In itself, it provides no purpose; it is a means toward the ends of life.

The human aspect, the building of our personal selves and our relationships, is the *essence* of life. It is the core process that is built on the physical base and uses the economic support.

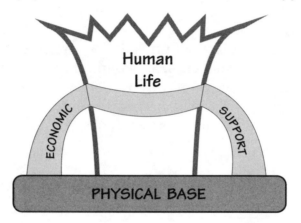

If we neglect or mismanage the physical aspect, we may not live as long or as vitally. If we ignore the economic aspect, we may be left without the essentials of care and comfort. If we neglect the human aspect, we may miss the essence of life and miss out on joy.

In making plans for the next year, what items do you include regarding physical issues, economic issues, and human issues? What does "quality of life" mean to you?

Decline and Emergence in Elderhood

In elderhood both physical energy and economic productivity are relentlessly declining, but human maturity is just as relentlessly pursuing its peak. This is the context of elderhood, and establishes its special quality.

Physical energy is decreasing.
Economic productivity is decreasing.
Human maturity is increasing.

It takes a lifetime to grow a full, mature, human person. It is a process that is never complete. Here are a few of the many human qualities that grow gradually throughout life:

♦ *Experience.* As we age we are exposed to more of life, and to different parts of life. The older we become, the more experience we accumulate.

♦ *Wisdom.* We process the experience of life and learn from it, especially from our mistakes.

♦ *Appreciation.* Elderhood is more a matter of love than it is of knowledge. The longer we live in the world, the more we appreciate it, embrace it, and fit in it comfortably. We care.

♦ *Wholeness.* We elders have already played many roles and developed many parts of ourselves. In elderhood we integrate all this past growth and form a full, complete, mature person.

There is always some emergent force in life, some expectant theme of vitality and meaning. To build on our strengths, we need to focus on what is emergent. This is true at any time, and in elderhood it is critical. Otherwise, we simply decide to decline.

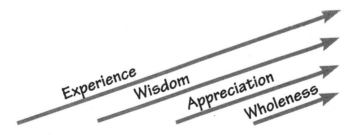

How important are your declines in physical and economic areas compared with your emergence in human qualities: wholeness, wisdom, caring, following your bliss?

Chapter 3

Our Cultural Bias

We live in a particular culture, so we are influenced not only by our personal view of aging, but also by the dominant attitude of our society about aging and old age.

Topics:

Our Young Roots

Life as Decline

Moving Beyond Physical Emphasis

The Price of Youth Bias

Realistic Decline

Elderhood and Medicine

Our Young Roots

Every culture builds attitudes about age and finds ways of dealing with elders, just as it does for children and for adults in midlife. Our culture places primary emphasis on the physical aspect of life. Second, it places emphasis on the economic aspect. It does not place as much emphasis on the human aspect at this time. Primarily, our social emphasis is that of youth. Our culture has a youth bias. We also respect the productive emphasis of midlife, but we have not yet discovered and embraced the human emphasis of elderhood.

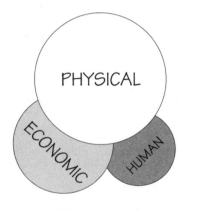 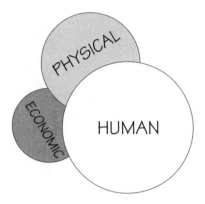

Where the culture is   Where elders are

The basis of ageism

This leads to cultural ageism. It is not so much that we elders are oppressed, but that we are discounted and under-valued. It could hardly be otherwise, for we are just beginning to value ourselves. We have not yet come "out of the closet."

. . . .

As you age, how do you experience ageism as discounting and under-valuing your life? Do you think there is something wrong with you or the culture?

Life as Decline

In a culture that idolizes youth, we see aging principally in physical terms. We view our course through life as a quick, short growth to the physical peak, followed by a long, gradual decline. The rise is coveted, the decline is avoided or denied. The beginning of life is a quick climb to physical perfection. The rest of life is seen as a long physical deterioration.

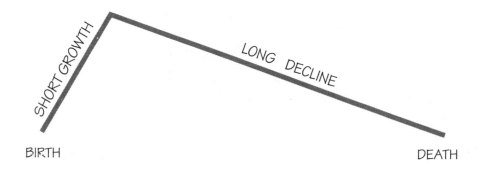

SHORT GROWTH

LONG DECLINE

BIRTH   DEATH

There are some serious implications of this decline view. Youth is valued and seen as our friend. Aging beyond the early twenties is despised and seen as our enemy. About one fifth to one quarter of life is seen as a process of growth; the rest of life is seen as a process of decay. If physical prowess is your only measure, most of life is seen in terms of loss. Life is lived as if it were a long, gradual process of dying.

The question is not whether this view is true or false, but whether it is complete and balanced. The sketch above represents, roughly, the growth and decline of physical energy and agility. It does not represent all of life. There is some truth to it as a view of the physical aspect, but it is a disaster to think of life in general as a process of deterioration. Yet in a culture that idolizes youth we are, in subtle ways, encouraged to do so.

. . . .

Our culture suggests that unless you are young and pretty, or young and Olympian, you are not worth much. To what extent have you accepted this? Do you accept it now? How would you change it?

Moving Beyond Physical Emphasis

Nothing is wrong with the physical view unless it is overemphasized or misplaced. In youth, a physical emphasis is fitting and useful. Its bias against age is secondary, for youth has only a dim view of age, and has little to do with it.

In midlife, physical emphasis is no longer very appropriate, for in midlife we are already past the physical peak. The youth bias begins to work against us.

In elderhood, the physical youth bias is depressing and destructive. It is counterproductive because it places high value on what we are losing, and sees little merit in age.

As we go through life we need to follow our strengths, and emphasize what we have to work with at the time. In youth we are bubbling with energy, so we emphasize that. In midlife our energy may be overextended, but we are flowing with productivity, which our culture also admires. It is easy to shift emphasis from the physical to the economic salient peak.

We elders are running short of physical energy and productivity, but are becoming more mature and closer to our essence. We need to shift our emphasis to this new area of available strength. It is more difficult to make this shift, because human maturity is not understood and valued, and our society does not offer or encourage a human agenda in age. We are left with the physical and the economic agendas, but if we accept them we rely on areas of weakness and decline. That is clearly a poor strategy.

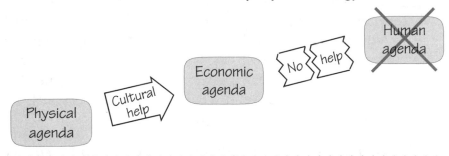

. . . .

To what extent do you rely on a physical agenda, an economic agenda, and a human agenda? Do you value all three? How does your human agenda make up for the predictable declines in the physical and economic areas?

The Price of Youth Bias

Overvaluing youth results in undervaluing age.

We pay both an individual and a collective price for our youth bias. Individually, we accept too naively an exaggerated view of physical decline as our model for life and aging. We place too little value on the growth that comes later in life, so we sell ourselves short. As we age, we need to reconsider whether we accept the decline view as a model for our own elderhood.

Remaining stuck in the bias of youth can lead to these problems:

♦ We may feel like victims, without control, as if we have no power or responsibility for rebuilding our lives or culture.

♦ We may feel that the meaningful part of life or history is behind us.

♦ The expectation of decline can become a self-fulfilling prophecy.

♦ If elders are not valued, they become wasted resources.

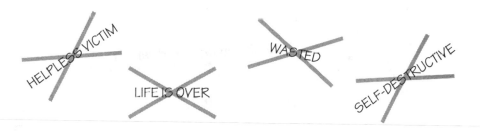

Don't buy deterioration as a model of elderhood.

. . . .

Will you cling to the decline view of aging which we inherited, or will you move beyond it? How can you eliminate ageism from your mind?

Realistic Decline

Physical energy fades and eventually we die. This cannot be denied. Facing the facts of physical decline and death is essential to successful elderhood.

Yet the decline we experience as we age generally turns out to be not as bad as we anticipate. Our expectations, influenced by our history, are far more terrible than the fact. The anticipation of decline is a projection of the fears of youth worshippers. It is not a factual description of the human prospect.

Short of serious disease, decline is usually experienced as a gradual slowing down, over several decades, with ample time to adjust.

Age brings increasing vulnerability to certain illnesses, and elders require good physical management and healthy habits. Given that, and short of accident or misfortune in the genetic lottery, most people can be healthy and active for most of their lifetimes. For most, serious deterioration can be delayed until close to the end. Then it is usually quite rapid, for it is part of the dying process.

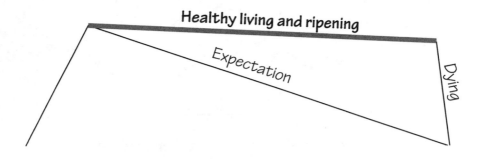

In successful elderhood, the business of deterioration comes at the end. Until then, the business of life is to live, not to die.

Decline is a gradual slowing down

· ·

What is your experience with physical decline? Is it as you expected? Is it manageable? How do you handle it in your mind?

Elderhood and Medicine

Just as we emphasize science, so we emphasize medicine, an art that is heavily dependent on supporting science. Medicine brings great benefits to elders. Its competence in the past has already lengthened our lives, and its competence in the present gives us some assurance of effective care when we need it.

But there are drawbacks. The focus of medicine is disease, not life, and not even health. It can help us survive and keep the physical system in repair—it does that job very well. It tells us little about how to live our elderhood, for that is not its area of expertise. Yet it is common in our culture to emphasize medical issues of aging. There are good reasons to consider these medical issues. Overemphasizing them, however, can make it seem as if aging is a branch of medicine, and elderhood is a disease.

Elderhood is not a disease!

Elderhood is a stage of life. It is not a disease any more than childhood is a disease. There are common physical problems in elderhood just as there are common childhood diseases. Elders may need their physicians more often because their bodies are wearing thin. Medical care is important in elderhood, but it does not define its essence.

While not denying the aches, pains, and diseases of elderhood, this book does not dwell on them. When they come, they make themselves felt all too strongly. They are a part of elderhood that is well known and already emphasized. We emphasize instead the lesser known and less appreciated parts of elderhood, the neglected richness.

. . . .

How do you use medicine to enhance your health without focusing on disease?

Chapter 4

From Retirement to Protirement

Our backward-looking view of retiring from work life needs to be replaced by a proactive view of moving forward into elderhood.

Topics:

Issues of Retirement

Abruptness of Retirement

The Value Bias on Work

Problems with Retirement

The Solution: Protirement

The Twin Tasks of Protirement

Issues of Retirement

The term "retirement" has several meanings, mostly related to leaving the phase of life structured around income-producing work. Most of us think of retirement in terms of financial issues such as:

If I have relied on income from my work for living expenses, what will I rely on now? Will pension and Social Security and investment income be enough?

What kind of life style do I want, and can I afford it?

How can I manage my money to make it last?

At a deeper level, retirement is a major life transition that brings us face to face with our aging. It forces us to deal with some of the issues of elderhood, such as:

If I have defined myself chiefly in terms of my work, and my work is gone, how do I define myself now?

If work has been the center of my life, what will the center be now?

If I have structured my daily activities chiefly in terms of my work, how will I structure them now?

Where do I go from here?

Retirement is a twentieth century American invention, not a developmental necessity. For some retirement is a gateway to elderhood. For others it is a disengagement from life itself.

. . . .

For you, what are the chief issues of retirement? What are its advantages and disadvantages?

Abruptness of Retirement

For most, the productive peak is around age 40, with a gradual buildup before and a gradual decline thereafter. In our culture, however, we think of productive economic activity in terms of entering or leaving employment in a job, business, or profession.

Many forms of work are highly technical or specialized, so there is a long period of education or preparation for work. Retirement, on the other hand, is usually an abrupt break with work as the central feature of life. So our productive careers tend to be "squared off" both at the beginning and at the end, and we tend to think of work life as follows:

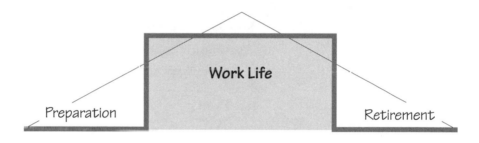

Economic career through life

The abruptness of retirement is a difficulty for many. Although our work commitments end suddenly, our work energy declines slowly and gradually. That energy needs to be applied in other ways.

The three phases of preparation, work, and retirement correspond loosely with youth, midlife, and elderhood. The event of retirement usually occurs at the time of life when one needs to plan for elderhood, and it can serve as a rite of passage into elderhood.

. . . .

What has your experience of retirement been, or what are your plans for it?

The Value Bias on Work

Money is one of our modern gods, second in line after Youth. We place great value on the working phase of life, when we are productive and making money. Since work is assigned high value, retirement is often assigned low value. The stages of life are valued like this:

This reflects the bias of midlife, which emphasizes the economic aspect. While this view is favorable for midlifers, it is clearly unfavorable for elders. It may be reasonable for midlifers to hold this view, but it is foolish for elders to hold it. Those who still hold it at retirement may feel lost after leaving work life, especially if they have not developed a positive view of elderhood.

As we age and come closer to death, we begin to see money as more transitory, and look for something more profound. We realize that the importance of life is in living, not in making a living. Our values shift gradually toward the human values that are discussed in this book. With a more human emphasis, elderhood looks more attractive.

We need a vision of elderhood with value.

Name three ways you can be more valuable five years from now.

Problems with Retirement

The word *retire* is so heavily laden with the negative connotation of withdrawal and loss that we feel the need to define a new word, *protire*, to denote a positive transition from work life into elderhood. To retire implies drawing back from the work life structures of the past and from the main stream of society; to protire implies leaping forward into the life flow of the future.

Retirement is sold in standardized packages; protirement must be individually designed. Retirement requires us to disengage from life as we have known it; protirement redirects our energies and carries our life work on to the next stage.

We may withdraw from a life style dominated by job, but we do not need to withdraw from life. Many who leave a work-centered life without a positive vision of a new phase do not long survive.

Detach from job, perhaps. Detach from life, no!

A chief hazard of retirement in our times is that, if we do not have a positive vision of the next phase of life, it may become a decline, a loss. It may seem like all ending and no beginning. We may feel like powerless victims, our identity stolen away, our value gone, and the meaning of life disappearing.

Retirement that hints of detachment from life is destructive.

Protirement that designs the next chapter of life is fulfilling.

. . . .

Do you know anyone who has suffered from retiring in the spirit of loss, retreat, and detachment from life? How might that person protire?

The Solution: Protirement

Protirement is life-oriented rather than work-oriented. In protirement we move into the future, building a new chapter of life by design, by intent, with energy, and with passion. We know where we are going, we like where we are going, and we are eager to move on. We are captain of our own ship, choosing our preferred future.

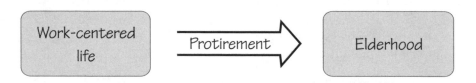

Protirement is a life transition, like many other transitions we have already gone through. It requires leaving one phase of life behind and moving on to another phase. It is not a withdrawal from life; it is a major change in life. Like other life transitions, it calls for adaptation and some redefinition of who we are in the next phase. It calls for vision, plans, and action. It may require new learning and new skills.

This summarizes the difference:

RETIREMENT	PROTIREMENT
Regressive, living in past	Proleptic, looking forward
Work-oriented	Life-oriented
Standardized	Individual design
Leaves value behind	Finds new value
Life is over	New phase of life
Powerless victim	By choice and design

- -

If you were to protire, what specific changes would you make in your life to grow into your fullness?

The Twin Tasks of Protirement

There are two major tasks of protirement:

- ◆ *Changing life structures.* Work imposes strong patterns on life. Everyday life style may be substantially changed as work-related structures are left behind or redefined, and new life structures are built to replace them.

- ◆ *Coming to terms with age.* Protirement from work creates another crisis: it forces us to face the issues of aging. This is one of its chief benefits.

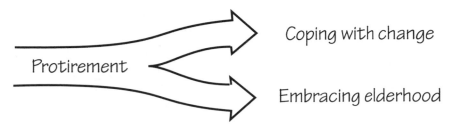

Protirement forces us to face the issues of age.

Protirement from full-time work is a wake-up call. It shakes us out of the long-standing patterns of midlife as if waking us from a sound sleep. It reminds us of many other things we would like to do, but have put aside because earning a living consumed most of our energy. It revives half-forgotten ambitions and ideals. It is a mixture of the loss of what is familiar and the rediscovery of possibilities. It forces us to examine our core values.

Protirement also reminds us that time is growing short and energy is waning. We must come to terms with age and with approaching death. Protirement is an invitation to turn the race against time into a planned journey.

If the twin tasks of protirement are approached concurrently and honestly, the situation changes in a profound way. The question is no longer "What will I do when I retire?" The question becomes "How shall I spend my elderhood in a fitting way?"

. . . .

Are you using protirement to embrace elderhood? How would you redesign your elder years as protirement? How would active engagement of your deepest values and concerns change your life style for the better?

Chapter 5

Living Longer

We have more years to live than our ancestors, and need a better idea of how to live them.

Topics:

    An Extra 25 Years

    The Role of Longevity

    The Pioneer Years

    Frontiers

An Extra 25 Years

Today we live about a quarter of a century longer than our grandparents did. Our culture has given us a marvelous gift! Some, however, see it as an extra burden.

Those of us who reach our sixties with health have good prospects for living on into the decades of our seventies, eighties, even nineties and beyond. These are years about which our culture has little experience, and against which it has a deep historical bias. These are years that are not considered useful, that are associated with decline, and that we have not yet learned to value.

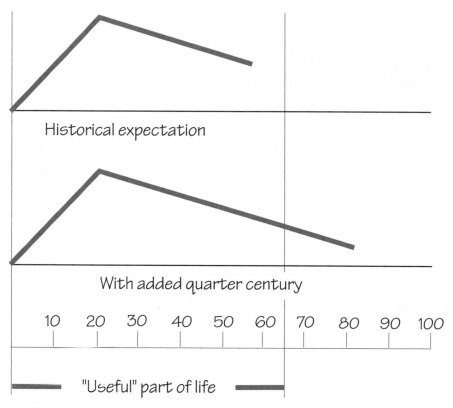

This is the modern challenge of elderhood. We are given an extra 25 years without good cultural prescriptions for how to spend it.

· ·

How long did your grandparents live? Your parents? How long do you expect to live? What is your sense of purpose as an elder? Write it out.

The Role of Longevity

Modern longevity is a stretching of our lifetimes, not just an appendage at the end of them. Our lives are not like those of our grandparents, with an extra 25 years tacked on; they differ throughout. We retain our vital energies longer than our forbears did.

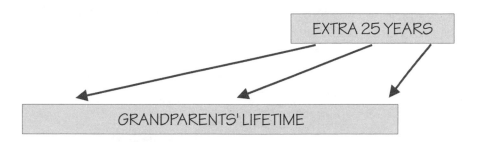

Try this fantasy: Suppose you could distribute your extra 25 years anywhere you choose in your lifetime. What phases of life would you stretch? Would you add elderhood?

This fantasy may clarify how you intend to use your extra years. There are three general approaches:

◆ *Stretching youth.* Fearing age, some cling to the trappings and myths of youth, emulating it even when they cannot regain it. They live their later years as a second childhood, dedicated to sport or fun or youthful pursuits.

◆ *Stretching midlife.* Some avoid or deny aging by remaining workaholics and seeing their value in production.

◆ *Stretching elderhood.* Some accept and embrace age, adopt age-appropriate values, and become elders, finding deep fulfillment and meaning.

If we focus on the physical or economic aspect, aging seems unattractive, and longevity is a robber which steals our energy and our productivity. If we focus on human development, longevity is a benefactor which gives us time to grow and to be.

. . . .

How are you planning to spend your extra 25 years? Sketch it out.

The Pioneer Years

There is no simple rule book for elderhood. This is unknown territory. We have made marvelous progress in extending the length of life, but little in exploring the quality of the added years. We are just starting to work on that, and we elders need to make it up as we go along. This is a demanding task, which requires imagination and perseverance. Perhaps that is one reason why many choose the regressive strategy of holding on to the earlier stages of life, which are more familiar.

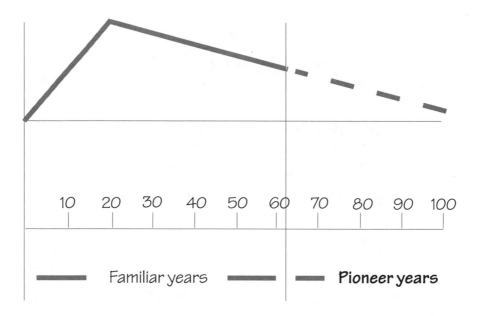

10 20 30 40 50 60 70 80 90 100

━━━ Familiar years ━━━ ┃ ━━━ **Pioneer years**

In our later years, we have more freedom and fewer external rules and guides than ever before. That freedom brings with it the challenge to design an elderhood that is uniquely fitting for us in these times. To be creative elders we cannot wait for someone to tell us what to do. We have to write our own script and shape our own future.

How do you feel about living a phase of life for which there is little precedent? Are you excited? Frightened? Both? Are you a pioneer?

Frontiers

There are many challenges in going into this pioneer territory. Each aspect of life presents a new frontier.

On the physical frontier, the most obvious challenge is survival. But survival alone is not enough. We want to survive under favorable conditions, in good health.

There are, of course, some physical hazards of age, and our extra 25 years will expose us to them. In facing these hazards we will probably do well, for we have vast experience and technology to help us.

On the economic frontier, we need to find new ways to use our creative and productive energy. These will be different from the frenetic ways of midlife. Even when protirement means that we leave gainful employment, it does not mean that we stop working in the broader sense. Our working energy does not suddenly stop, but we do need a new vision of "work" in age.

The human frontier is the most important but, in modern times, the least known. We have little experience in growing to human fullness in age. This frontier is explored in this book.

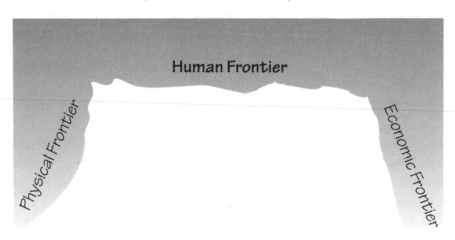

In particular, we need a plan of exploration. Our culture offers us the extra years without a clear purpose or mission. Unless we find suitable purpose for those extra years, we may lose some of them.

. . . .

Tentatively, what is your mission as an elder? Write it out.

Part II
Becoming a More Complete Person

Age has a poor reputation largely because it is unknown or misunderstood. In our youthful society, age has, in effect, been graded by youngsters, whose view of age tends to be both unrealistic and dismal. This is the basis of our ageism.

Successful elderhood requires a more positive view of aging; we need to look at the process of aging with new eyes. Towards that end, this part considers selected aspects of the process of human development and maturing in the later years.

Chapter 6
Perspectives of Aging

There are many ways to look at aging, and our perspective changes as we move through life. This chapter looks at this changing process from several viewpoints.

Topics:

> The Vessels of Life
>
> Proleptic Youth, Regressive Age
>
> Bubble Vision
>
> Surprise in Aging
>
> Looking Back at Life
>
> The Appearance of Age

The Vessels of Life

Our passage through life is like an ocean voyage. We are always underway and moving, but in different ways and, as it were, in different vessels.

Youth is a roaring speedboat, skimming across the surface of life, leaving a turbulent wake, showing its speed.

Midlife is a ponderous, heavily-laden cargo ship, efficiently plowing the shipping lanes on regular schedule, delivering the goods.

Elderhood is a graceful sailing vessel, sails billowing in the breeze, sailing where it will.

Elderhood is not spent in dry-dock but on the high seas. It is not spent skimming over the surface at high speed, close to shore. Nor is it spent plowing the shipping lanes in predetermined, straight course. It is an adventure of discovery on the high seas of life.

How much of your life is still like a speedboat or freighter? How can you design a life like a graceful sailing vessel? Find an elder who has accomplished this and ask how it was done.

Proleptic Youth, Regressive Age

Young people are eager to "grow up"; adults are reluctant to grow up more. A child, asked *How old are you?* is likely to tell you how old he or she will be on the next birthday. *I'm going on seven.* This is still true in the teens. *I'm almost sixteen. I'll soon have my driver's license.*

After the early twenties—the perfect age—there is a shift. The question *How old are you?* is no longer polite to ask. We act as if there is no more growing up to do, as if the direction is down from there on. Persons as young as thirty start talking of being "over the hill." We know one man who received a black funeral crepe as a fortieth birthday gift!

Youth sees aging as a positive adventure. Most young people anticipate what is coming, and take joy in life yet to be lived. This outlook can be called *proleptic*—one of the meanings of that word is "leaping ahead." Most youths are proleptic, leaping ahead in their physical growth and aging. They see where they are going and are eager to get there. This is a healthy attitude, one which spurs us on, builds energy, promotes joy, and leads to success.

In a world of youth idolatry, we easily lose our proleptic quality after the first peak, and become regressive, looking back toward the peaks already passed. Proleptic youth turns too easily into regressive midlife, then into desperately regressive old age.

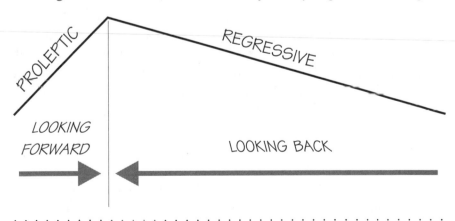

How do you feel about being your present age? Do you readily reveal your age? Are you looking forward to your next birthday?

Bubble Vision

We cannot climb all of life's peaks at once, so we concentrate on the part of the trail we are hiking at the time. At any age, we tend to build our own local bubbles and to live within them. It is easy to surround ourselves with cohorts of our own age, to become absorbed in our common issues, to speak our local vocabulary, and to neglect or ignore whatever is outside our bubble.

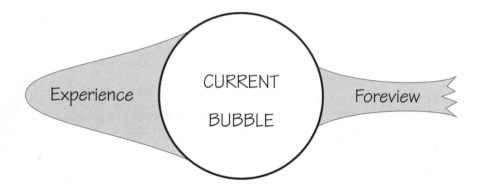

We see clearly within our bubble. We may see behind us through our experience. But it is more difficult to see where we are going. We go through life as if walking or driving through a fog, seeing only a short distance ahead. In this sense, aging is a blind process.

Living in their own bubbles, youths and midlifers cannot see far enough ahead to know and understand age. Even elders cannot see ahead clearly. Just as the youth of 15 wonders what it will be like to be 25, and the midlifer of 45 wonders what it will be like to be 55, so the elder of 75 wonders what it will be like to be 85. And the ultimate blindness is that we cannot see beyond death.

We do not know any age until we reach it.

. . . .

What do you think your life will be like in 10 years? How well can you foresee it?

Surprise in Aging

One common factor in looking ten years ahead is that, subjectively, it seems *old*. We distort the time scale of life as we go through it so that our present age seems natural and normal and O.K., but a few years later seems old and terrible—until we reach it. We might call this Murphy's Law of Age Perception: At any given age, ten years older seems old.

We do not fully understand any age until we reach it, then what we find is often not what we expected. Compared with our pessimistic expectations, the reality of age often turns out to be a pleasant surprise, if ageism has not already turned life sour.

As we age and gather more experience, our bubble tends to increase in size. We elders can live in a bigger bubble, if we remember and learn from our experience.

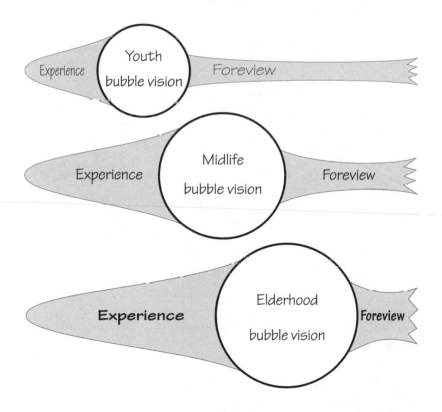

Has Murphy's Law of Age Perception applied to you in past decades? Does it apply now? Is your bubble increasing in size?

Looking Back at Life

In the practice of youth idolatry, our god is about 21 years old—that is about the perfect age. In later years, one would expect, we should look back with nostalgia to the time of our early twenties and wish we were back there again.

But it doesn't turn out that way. In surveys in which older people are asked which time of life is the best, youth is seldom the winner. Few want to relive the pain of childhood, the turbulence of adolescence, and the struggles to "make it." Looking back, midlifers tend to choose about 35, before wrinkles and disillusionment set in. Oldsters tend to pick the 50s or 60s. As our population ages, the preferred age may go still higher.

QUALITY PEAK

30s ➡   50s ➡ 60s ➡

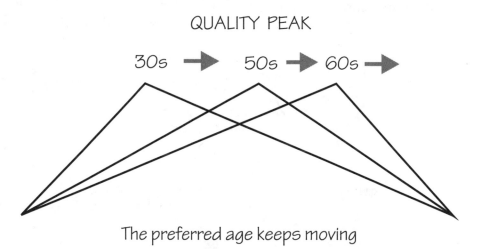

The preferred age keeps moving

Youth disdains age, but when age is graded by older people, the results are different. Elders prefer the more mature years.

. . . .

Looking back, what is the best period of your life? Looking ahead, what will get better?

The Appearance of Age

For many, the most difficult part of aging is the way we look. We idolize the appearance of youth, and have not yet learned to appreciate and enjoy the appearance of age. In this sense also, we do not see the center of the geode. We have ingrained appreciation for the young body, but little for the character of age.

To younger people, older people look strange, even offensive, for they are reminders of their own fears of aging. In midlife we look in the mirror and see our father's or mother's face, and we are shocked. It offends us that we could look like that. We start out wanting to look like Shirley Temple and end up looking more like Yoda. The mirror becomes our enemy.

We have not, men or women, learned to appreciate and build inner beauty, and to replace the fleeting beauty of youth with a more enduring type. Those who manage to do so are strikingly attractive people at any age.

We do not see our bodies as others do. Our bodies are our personal displays, announcing clearly who we are. They record and advertise our human growth, or the lack of it. Albert Camus has said that by 40 everyone has the face he deserves. Our faces record our character for all to see. The world knows us and traces our progress, often even better than we know ourselves.

After 40, growth goes on, and our faces continue to record it. We also have the face we deserve at 60, and at 80. Our body not only records our physical weakening, it also proclaims our spiritual growth.

. . . .

Look in the mirror with new eyes and see who you are and whom you are becoming. Select a photograph of yourself that you are proud of, and put it where you will see it every day. Keep looking behind the obvious for the spiritual depth.

Chapter 7

Aging as Development

Successful aging calls for timely and fitting emergence, adding value as we go. We change radically in this process, if we keep moving on.

Topics:

Lifelong Development

Age and Maturity

The Elder

Age Adds Worth

Re-ranking of Values in Age

Age is Value-Driven

The Seasons of Life

The Arrested Person

The Challenge of Moving On

Lifelong Development

Academically, the development of youth has been studied extensively, while development of adults, especially healthy elders, has been neglected until recently. Strangely, we have viewed adults and elders as if they were beyond development, as if our development stops when we reach adulthood. We now know that is not the case.

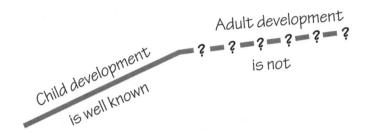

We have carefully studied the physical and medical factors of aging, but not the human factors. As we start to study the characteristics of development in midlife and elderhood, we are finding an unsuspected variety and richness. Gradually we are forming an idea of lifelong development.

Lifelong emergence is a possibility, not a requirement. As we age, we have some options. We can foster growth, postpone it, or avoid it.

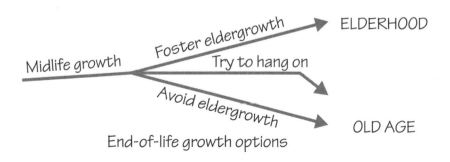

End-of-life growth options

. . . .

Did you stop developing when you reached adulthood, or have you continued since then? Are you still developing? How?

Age and Maturity

Age is one measure of life; maturity is another. Age measures the number of times the earth has revolved around the sun since you were born; maturity measures how you are emerging as a human being.

We age at a fixed rate, which we cannot control. We mature at a varying rate, which we can control to some extent. A chief theme of this book is that we continue to mature throughout life. At any age, we can continue to become more fully human.

The rate at which we mature in the human sense is uneven because youth, midlifers, and elders live in different personal worlds. Roughly speaking, emergence is rapid during youth, somewhat slower when we are distracted by the affairs of midlife, and again rapid during elderhood.

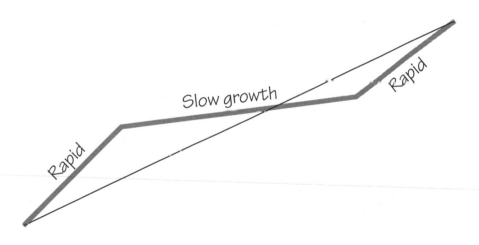

Our culture does not invite us to the final spurt of development in elderhood, for it expects us to be fading instead of developing. We are only recently starting to realize that late growth is natural, and we hardly know what to do with it.

. . . .

Do you think that you can continue to develop, perhaps even rapidly, in your elder years? Describe what you think is possible.

The Elder

In successful development, the full and mature person that eventually emerges is the *elder*. The state of life in which this fullness is enjoyed is elderhood.

An elder is not merely a person who has reached some chronological age such as 65. Rather, an elder is one who has lived through youth and learned its lessons, has lived through midlife and learned its lessons, and has matured into the third major phase of life. It is a matter of forged and evolved development rather than age. If we reach elderhood, our purpose in life shifts and our way of life changes.

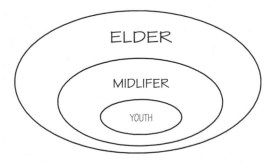

Just as midlife includes the experience and learning of youth, but expresses it in a new way, so elderhood embraces both youth and midlife, and goes beyond them. There is still a Youth part and a Midlifer part within the Elder, but they are now integrated into a full person and expressed in a mature way.

In elderhood we start living as more complete persons. We enjoy a human fullness that is not yet possible in youth, and that we cannot quite reach in midlife. There is a subtle, gradual change from the narrower, productive focus of midlife to a broader, more inclusive human attitude. We pursue connectedness and wholeness. We say what we believe. We live to live.

The elder grows closer to the essence of humanness, beyond the ignorance and masks and busyness of younger years. This is a great change, and a climactic one.

. . . .

How do you sense elderhood or the growth toward it in yourself? What qualities are you growing as an elder? How does your agenda connect to others and to the culture?

Age Adds Worth

For humans, development is change with added value. Life is like an investment whose value increases with time. In the human sense, our worth is cumulative. Our development as adults is based upon what we have already developed in youth, and adds to it. Similarly, our continuing development in elderhood is built on the base we have already constructed in youth and midlife. In age we complete the building of our selves. We keep on adding value.

Aging is a value-added process.

Our priorities change as we age, but the process of adding value goes on. Our focus changes, but growth continues, and personal worth increases. We reach our peak in elderhood.

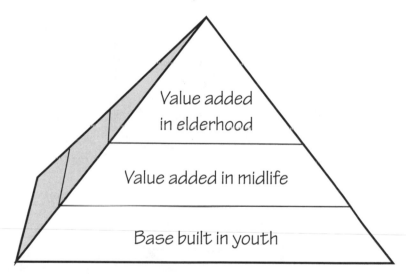

The kind of value we add is influenced by what we hold most precious at the time. Youths are likely to measure their worth in physical terms. Midlifers are likely to calculate their "net worth" in economic terms. Elders measure their worth in human terms, and add human value to themselves, their families, and their communities. If we focus only on physical worth or economic worth, we see decline, and may miss this increase of human worth.

· ·

What of value did you add to yourself in youth? In midlife? What of value are you adding in elderhood?

Re-Ranking of Values in Age

We adjust our values as we age, re-ranking them to fit our station in life and our growing maturity. In midlife, values such as productivity, acquisition, and personal power may rank near the top. It is a time to *do*. In age these values may lose some of their importance and be replaced by others such as intimacy, family relationships, and spirituality. Elderhood is a time to *be*.

The change is like that of a ship going through a lock that separates waters of different levels. The lock is a place of transition. The ship enters at one level and leaves at another, but not until the sluice valves allow water from the higher level to flow into the lock and gradually raise the level of the ship to that of its destination waters.

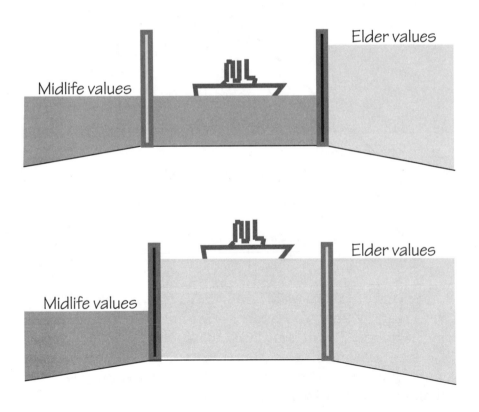

What values do you rank highest in this phase of your life? Write them out.

Age is Value-Driven

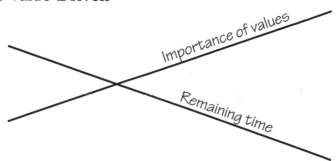

The impact of values intensifies with age. As the remainder of life shortens, we tend to be dedicated only to those things we value most highly. Values move to center stage. We sense that we are running out of time, so we prioritize better. We choose our heart's top values, and are less willing to spend limited energy on secondary values. Midlifers are willing to spend far more energy than they can easily muster in running a business and earning a dollar. Elders no longer hold money and that form of success among the highest values. Elders choose values that will outlive them.

To age self-consciously is to become value-driven.

The value drive of elders is quite different from the productive drive of midlifers. It does not attempt to overwhelm a task through sheer effort and activity. It is calm but intense, unhurried but persistent, fueled internally rather than externally. Yet it is transcendent, seeking connections to the world around us. This energy is at the core of elderhood and must be used. At its best it is ecstatic, radiant, and peaceful energy.

It is important for us elders to be clear about our values and to know how they are changing. If the lock gate of midlife is closed behind us, yet we never get around to sluicing in the waters of elderhood and opening the lock gate ahead of us, we become stuck in the lock and stagnant.

. . . .

What is most important to you in age? Are there things you were eager to do earlier that you no longer want to spend time on? Are there things you have always wanted to do or be that make good sense for this time of your life?

The Seasons of Life

Ecclesiastes says that for everything and everyone, there is a season. In life, there is a season for youth, a season for midlife, and a season for elderhood. Ideally, we flow through the seasons of life smoothly, just as time marches through the seasons of the year. Successful persons flow with the seasons, riding with them like a surfer. We flow from the blossoming of springtime to the fullness of summer, then the harvest, the splendor and fading of autumn, and the death of winter. A successful person loves all the seasons, and is content to flow with them.

YOUTH	MIDLIFE	ELDERHOOD
Springtime years	Summer and harvest	Autumn and winter

Well-timed transitions

It does not go so smoothly for everyone. We can be reasonably confident that a person of fifteen will have the station in life and attitude toward life of a youth. It is likely that a person of forty-five will have the station and attitude of a midlifer, but it is not a sure bet. And it is not at all a sure bet that a person of seventy has adopted the station and attitude of an elder.

Elderhood is not forced upon us. All of us grow old, many of us become retirees or pensioners, but fewer of us become elders.

As an attitude toward life, elderhood can come early, late, or never. Most of us do not know this attitude until we are deep into midlife and sense the inevitability of death in a profound way. Yet a youth who is threatened by fatal illness may become a precocious elder, driven to bring some form of closure to life in an untimely way.

Our culture sings the praises of spring and summer, and attends the harvest. It neglects autumn and winter.

. . . .

How will you celebrate all of your seasons? What positive features attend your autumn and winter?

The Arrested Person

There are two common ways that people become stuck in the past and simply grow old rather than become elders. They can be called *eternal midlife* and *eternal youth*.

Eternal midlifers cling to the plateau, often sagging, that they reached in midlife. Seeing little value in elderhood, they continue to define themselves in terms of their work, their productivity, their money, and their possessions. Often workaholics to the end, they continue to turn the midlife crank beyond the time when it is appropriate to become elders. They die as old midlifers.

YOUTH	MIDLIFE	STILL MIDLIFE
Early years	Middle years	Later years

Eternal midlife

Eternal youths continue to define themselves primarily in terms of their physical prowess. They remain ego driven and unaware of deeper callings. They are more concerned about their appearance than their meaning.

YOUTH	STILL YOUTH	STILL YOUTH
Early years	Middle years	Later years

Eternal youth

Eternal midlifers and eternal youths are both swayed by the popular view of age, which sees elderhood as decline. They lack a vision for the rest of their human agenda. They become stuck, waiting to be born to the rest of life.

. . . .

How would you describe the advantages of a healthy, growing elderhood to an eternal midlifer? To an eternal youth?

The Challenge of Moving On

Youth is vital, midlife is vital, and elderhood is vital. But the basic agenda of each is different, the station in life is different, and the values are different. A problem occurs when one clings to an outworn agenda when it no longer fits, and is stuck there. It is neither natural nor productive to stand in one phase of life wishing we were in another.

To leap forward to the next peak, we must see that there is something ahead worth reaching. If we cannot see the road ahead getting any better, we are tempted to live in the past, in denial or in passive resignation. Unless we see age as a value-adding part of our journey, it is difficult to move on, so we demote ourselves and put our lives on the shelf.

So many people make the mistake of assuming that successful elderhood lies in retaining the physical energy of youth and the productive energy of midlife. Of course, it is desirable to retain them as best we can, but that is not the chief focus of elderhood.

We do not reject youth, we outgrow it. The values and activities of youth may seem somewhat superficial in elderhood. We do not reject midlife—we appreciate it. It has served us well, and we did our part as we passed through. Now we can see it from a distance, in perspective, as a lopsided lifestyle.

The real success of elderhood is not in retaining the past, but in moving on to the future. *The challenge in entering elderhood is to gain the maturity, wisdom, and human energy of age without losing the playfulness of youth and the dreams and activity of midlife.*

If you were reaching a rich elderhood this year, what would the ingredients be? How would you sustain the playfulness of youth and the activity of midlife?

Chapter 8

Emergence of the Full Person

In the second half of life, growth is different, not just more of the same. Just as the agenda we formed in childhood is reaching fruition, a new agenda emerges, and a new and fuller phase of life begins.

Topics:

The Richness of Experience

"Making It" in Age

Life Begins at 40

The Second Maturing

The Radar of Age

The Mastery of Age

The Richness of Experience

Some things are lost with age, but more things are gained. In the human sense—the sense that is now most important—we grow richer. We feel more comfortable with life.

The riches of elderhood are not measured in terms of dollars, luxurious houses, and RVs. Some elders may have these things also, but they are not the criteria of wealth in age. Since we elders have switched our priority from the economic to the human, we must look to what we have collected that is of human value.

In age we make the wonderful discovery that our reservoir of experience is very full. We will add yet more, but it is not urgent to do so. Since we already have so much, we work with what we have, and we switch our emphasis from quantity to quality.

It is as if we go through life carrying all our experience with us in a backpack. By elderhood our backpack is brimming with experience, some of it integrated, and some of it distilled into wisdom. We are prepared; we have with us what we need to deal with whatever facets of life we encounter along the trail.

In youth we have great energy and enthusiasm, but little to work with. In age we have a great deal more to draw from. We have something important to say.

. . . .

What do you carry in your backpack of experience? What have you learned that urges you toward the depth and breadth of life? How can you share your experience fruitfully with the culture around you?

"Making It" in Age

Life is like a soup that improves with age. Youth is a fresh broth, lightly cooked. Midlife is a thicker soup, with many more ingredients thrown in. Elderhood is a hearty stew, with the flavors well blended and married. All are good; each is different.

Earlier in life we look forward to "making it" by reaching some milestone. We anticipate that when we move from adolescence to productive adulthood we will have "made it." But it does not turn out that way; we find that adulthood brings new problems. When we are married and have children—but marriage and parenthood bring new responsibilities, problems, and restrictions. When we own a fancy house—but the house brings a big mortgage. When we get that big promotion, or become CEO—but being CEO brings a rat race.

In elderhood we no longer depend on reaching some external goal to "make it." Whether we have realized our youthful ambitions is no longer as important as it once was. By now we have tasted both success and failure, and used them both in our growth.

In another sense, we have already "made it" by surviving all the trials and adventures of youth and midlife, and reaching an advanced age in reasonably good condition.

Along the way, our attention gradually shifts from outer to inner, and from the goals to the process of becoming. We become more attuned to the here and now, to life's journey day by day. Our ambition is to be awake and present and caring in the moment. We no longer put off "making it" until we reach some goal. In that sense, we have already arrived at where we want to be.

Living in such a process, we gradually emerge as full persons. The process is ongoing and never finished. We are always emerging, never fully emerged. Life is a work of art in progress.

How are you like a work of art in progress? What is complete and what is seeking completeness?

Life Begins at 40

The expression *Life begins at 40* may seem like a bluff in youth. Yet it contains truth that most of us do not discover until we reach that age or pass it. Before 40, most of us seem still somehow incomplete. We are still busy discovering who we are and gathering experience. Sometime in the 40s, we finish the job of collecting all our parts, and they start to work together as a full set. Then a maturity of personality starts to emerge. In elderhood it is sufficiently emerged that we simply enjoy being who we are.

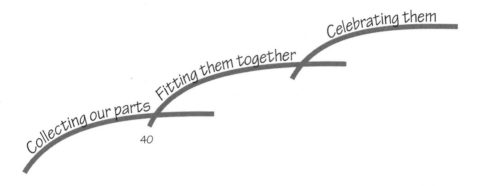

Sometime in their 40s, most people experience the birth of fullness, the beginning of the second half of life. As the saying suggests, the 40s are only the beginning of the fullness of life. Two decades later, in early elderhood, the process takes over more of our attention, and becomes the central focus of our lives.

It takes decades for the full self to develop and emerge. As it gradually emerges, less of our energy goes into projecting an image, and more of it goes into expressing our essence. Our unique personality begins to emerge in its full scope, and in its own style. We are less willing to play roles, more eager to be ourselves. The transition may be rocky, with troubled periods, notably those called midlife crises.

. . . .

Do you remember a time in your life when you got all your parts together and started to live in a new way? Where are you in your life-long emergence of selfhood? What critical tasks do you need to attend to now, to keep growing?

The Second Maturing

In the first half of life we live from the outside in as we collect our parts and build ourselves. We are guided by others to the best choices. Healthy people want to transcend external measures of their lives. They seek internal measures deep within their own beliefs and values. They begin to live from the inside out.

First half:
Living from the Outside In

Second half:
Living from the Inside Out

In elderhood we make an art of living from the inside out. We keep pursuing a complete human imprint, with internal origin and measures. We devote ourselves to growing the Full Person we are capable of becoming.

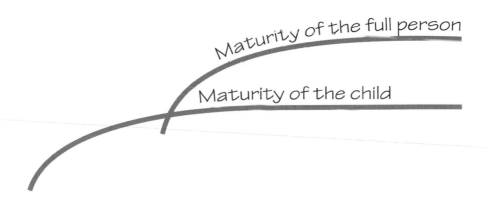

Maturity of the full person

Maturity of the child

When the full human imprint functions, there is a rebirth. A new phase of life starts, which grows to maturity in elderhood. We rediscover the spirit of development that we knew earlier in a primitive and unselfconscious way. Now we know it in a conscious, deliberate, mature way. We become more interested in integration and transcendence than in money and work.

Have you experienced a shift from a Child-driven to a Full Person-driven life? At about what age? What was it like?

The Radar of Age

The sailing vessel of elderhood is equipped with good radar. We have the antenna of our awareness, the holistic computer of our mind, and the vast data base of our experience. As we explore the ocean of age, we have broad and effective vision. We can pick up the signals and we know how to interpret them.

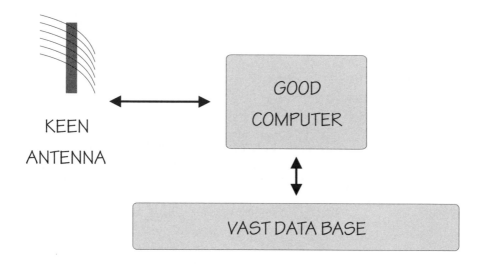

The computer may seem slow, but that is partly because the data base is so large. There is much experience to look through. That is part of the burden of age.

We do not need to look through all of it. In age, we have already put many of the pieces of the puzzle of life into place. We can see more of the picture, and it becomes easier to fit in the remaining pieces. On the other hand, we now want a global and holistic picture, so the puzzle is no longer as simple. For any new input, we have many more links. For any topic there are more reference points. We can shift perspective and see more aspects. Yet all of this processing of references and links and aspects is not important in itself but only as it leads to our goal of a unified picture of the whole.

· ·

Have you perfected your radar? Do you perceive data and process it differently from when you were younger? In what ways?

The Mastery of Age

As we age we learn how to do more things, and we learn how to do them better. We gain mastery—the embodiment of know-how and the incorporation of knowledge into life style.

There is a progression in our learning how to do things. We must first learn deliberately and consciously, guiding and monitoring our activity, trying different approaches until we gain *conscious competence*—we know how to do it when we think about it. Later, we may do the same thing so often that it becomes habitual. Our competence becomes embodied, built into our firmware. Then we have *unconscious competence*, for we can perform without having to think about it. The know-how seems to be available in our cells.

The older we get, the more things we can do without thinking about it. We gain more unconscious competence. Especially, we reach competence in human affairs—we operate in a mature way by habit. Our intuition is good. We can size up others better than before. We can handle ourselves and our relationships. In difficult situations we have a good base to start from; for example, we have been through enough quarrels that we know how to manage ourselves better than earlier. We have been through many crises and transitions in life. We know the territory and can see the patterns.

What are some ways that you are unconsciously competent in human affairs?

Chapter 9

Completion

Elderhood brings a need for and sense of completion. That does not mean closing down. Rather, it is a time for wrapping up, for making sense of our life story and making it complete. As death draws nearer, we feel an urgency to finish the job while there is still time.

Topics:

Finishing the Tapestry of Life

The Thirst for Wholeness

The Late Bloomer

Aliveness in Elderhood

Integrity

A Strategy for Wholeness

The Shadow of Age

The Chiaroscuro of Age

The Wisdom of Age

Finishing the Tapestry of Life

Life is like weaving a beautiful tapestry. It is not a linear tapestry of simple warp and woof, on which we start at one end and work straight through to the other end. Rather, it is like a web, on which we can work here and there as we please. We plan our tapestry early and revise it as we age, thoroughly elaborating the design in some areas and merely sketching other areas.

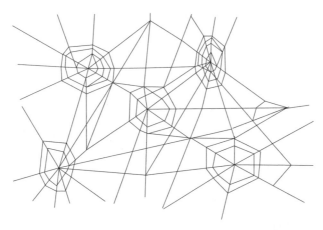

In youth we can play with the design, for there is ample time to experiment. It seems as if weaving the tapestry could go on forever. But as the shadow of death gradually approaches, there comes a day when we say to ourselves: "I've got to finish this darn tapestry! I can't leave these threads for others to finish, and I may not have very long to do it. There's no time to waste. I've got to finish my tapestry."

It's not that there is a rush—rushing is for midlife. But there is a no-nonsense focusing on the task. And there is a strong desire to do a good job of weaving. We realize that our tapestries are the summing up of the meaning of our lives, and the greatness of our lives.

Finishing the tapestry is a very appropriate activity for elders. It is a challenging and exciting activity, and gives the lie to the fiction of elderhood as nothing but loss and dying.

. . . .

Which parts of your tapestry are you satisfied with? Which need more work? Do you feel the need to finish your tapestry at this time?

The Thirst for Wholeness

Looking at our tapestry, we may see that it is good, but unevenly done. Some parts may seem overwrought, bristling with threads; others may seem sketchy or hardly touched, lacking color. Then we realize that the tapestry is our own, and is a highly personal work of art. We look at one part with great satisfaction and pride. We look at one sketchy part and decide it's O.K. as it is. We look at another sketchy part and say, "I want to finish that part."

Earlier, we have lived parts of life and neglected others, and have built parts of ourselves and not others. Now it is time to live some of the life we put aside, to build some of the parts that we did not get around to earlier, and to pull it all together.

Elderhood is a holistic time; the emphasis is on wholeness. When we work on a part it is because that part is necessary to achieve wholeness; we do not feel complete without it. We want to broaden ourselves where we feel narrow, and deepen ourselves where we feel shallow. It is a time for the emergence of neglected parts that are ready and willing to emerge—those parts that yearn to be expressed in this lifetime to make us whole.

The parts
of youth

The whole
of age

Wholeness is never fully achieved, and it takes decades to approach. In the turmoil of youth and the grinding demands of midlife, it is neglected, lost, or postponed. It takes half a lifetime to see wholeness as a real mission and the other half to partially achieve it. Wholeness becomes a central challenge in elderhood.

Wholeness is a goal rather than a clearly definable state. It cannot be reached for it is too vast, but it can be approached, and that is enough. Pursuing it is very satisfying.

How concerned were you with wholeness in your youth? How concerned are you now? How do you seek wholeness?

The Late Bloomer

Some people bloom early, in the sense of achieving a peak of success early in life. Others may be lackluster in earlier life, but blossom later. Or, if they have blossomed earlier, they blossom again, usually in a different way. Early bloomers reach their peaks amidst the values of youth or midlife. More often than not, they measure their success in physical or financial terms. Late bloomers emerge amidst the more mature values of elderhood.

The blossom of youth is simpler, like a daisy. The blossom of age is more subtle; it has more depth, more dimensions. Like a rose, it seems to be beyond dimension.

The late bloom emerges, or reemerges, from a richer soil, nurtured by the wisdom extracted from decades of experience, watered by the joys of much living, and fertilized by untold failure, disappointment, and pain.

The late bloomer should be appreciated as a rose. There is nothing to be gained by flattening out the petals of the rose and trying to make it into a daisy.

. . . .

Do you think most of us have the capacity to be late bloomers in some area? Do you? In what areas?

Aliveness in Elderhood

In one sense, elderhood is more demanding than youth or midlife. Earlier life presents tasks of growing and doing; elderhood presents talks of being. It calls for more aliveness, more consciousness, than any earlier age.

This demand for aliveness in elderhood is not foreseen when we are young, and we may be surprised by it. *This is the treachery of elderhood in our times: We expect dullness and inactivity; instead we find greater aliveness and challenge. We expect to retire and we get a wake-up call.*

In one sense it is the same, familiar call for alertness and aliveness that we have heard often before in life. Earlier we could more easily ignore it, now it has a new urgency and authority.

Although it is a compelling call to wake up and become more alive, we can ignore it if we choose. High consciousness is natural in elderhood, but it may be unfamiliar, and achieving it can be hard work. We can insist on a lower level of consciousness, or on unconsciousness if we choose. Alcohol is a popular way to do so.

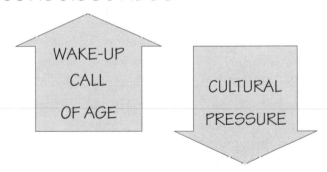

CONSCIOUSNESS

WAKE-UP CALL OF AGE

CULTURAL PRESSURE

UNCONSCIOUSNESS

We need to be aware that we are programmed by our culture for depression and despair in age. If we accept that programming, unconsciousness seems like an attractive sedative. If we reject that programming, wake up and accept the challenge of elderhood, we will need all the aliveness we can muster.

. . . .

In the space between aliveness and unconsciousness, where do you choose to be? How do you get to be there?

Integrity

According to the classical view of the psychologist Erik Erikson, the task of old age is to achieve integrity—to put life experience together in one's own style. One who succeeds in doing this builds wisdom. One who fails to do it satisfactorily ends in despair.

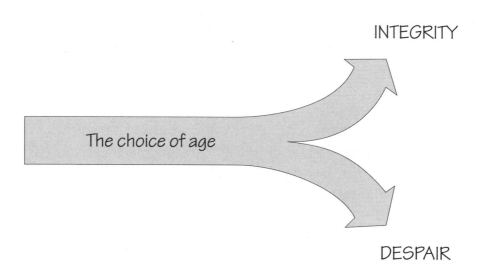

INTEGRITY

The choice of age

DESPAIR

An elder with integrity is one who has grasped the important parts of self and has blended them into one consistent, unique person.

Integration is the summing of a lifetime. The integrated person carries all of his or her past life along and gives it unified meaning. In the integrated person, what was black and white takes on color. Success and failure are included with equal respect. Reason cohabits intimately with emotion.

In this way elders become more fully human. Integrity becomes a way of life. Life becomes simpler and deeper.

While the physical system is falling apart, the self is coming together.

. . . .

What elements of your life are now coming together with integrity?

A Strategy for Wholeness

In age we have both the leisure and the urge to do some of the things we always wanted to do but never got around to. Most people understand this in terms of travel and hobbies, but it applies also, and especially, to personal emergence.

In seeking wholeness, we find aspects of ourselves that are still rough, unfinished, even undiscovered. Despite our maturity, we sense parts within us that are still gestating and yearning to be born. As we shift to human values, some of the holes within ourselves become more apparent, and we want to fill them.

Having outgrown midlife, we are no longer satisfied turning the same old crank. We want to take off the blinders, look around, and ask ourselves, "Are there parts of my life that seem incomplete? Are there core passions that are frustrated?"

In pursuit of wholeness, a good strategy for elders is: *Emphasize what has been neglected.*

A shift of values always brings up neglected areas. How much one finds is an individual matter; it may be little or it may be great. There is no check list of things we must do, and no general pattern to which we must conform. Life is not a paint-by-the-numbers exercise, but an individual work of art.

When we find a neglected area, choosing to work on it is an individual matter. Two elements are needed to move us: it must be personally important to us and we must have a strong inner urge to do it.

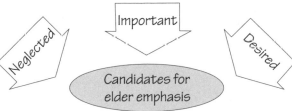

. . . .

What do you feel you have neglected in life? Which neglected parts do you want to pursue in your remaining years? In your notebook, divide a page into two columns labeled as below, and build a list of candidates.

Before I die I want to DO: Before I die I want to BE:

The Shadow of Age

A strange thing happens to elders. Driven by the thirst for wholeness, we start to include in our lives not only things we earlier neglected, but also things we outright rejected.

The psychology of Carl G. Jung speaks of the idea of *shadow*—those parts of our personality that we deny or reject, those parts of ourselves that we do not love. We tend to see those parts in others rather than in ourselves.

In youth it is easy to live in a good-and-bad, black-and-white world. Much of life, including parts of our own personality, gets conveniently classified as all good or all bad. So we build up a lot of shadow, a lot of ourselves that we reject.

Elderhood is a gray age, and we cannot so glibly classify things in black-and-white terms. We look between black and white and find, to our surprise and delight, all the colors of the rainbow. The world becomes richer and more real. As our hair becomes gray, our personalities develop more color.

Looking back from the mature vantage point of age, some of our earlier assumptions and attitudes seem thin and simplistic. We realize we have been living some parts of life as if it were a John Wayne western movie. In the search for wholeness we start to embrace what we earlier rejected. Internally, we welcome home a few prodigal sons, and the family gets richer and more powerful through their presence.

In retrospect, we discover that the rejected parts of ourselves have a value that we overlooked. Cutting out parts of our personality turns out to be a kind of psychic surgery that leaves us maimed. Later in life we need to gather back some rejected parts and integrate them into our more mature selves.

What are some of your shadow parts?

The Chiaroscuro of Age.

Elderhood is like a billowing tree in the bright sunshine. One sees a thousand points of light (to borrow a phrase from a past president) caught by the sun, and also a thousand points of shadow where the sun does not reach. In painting, the term *chiaroscuro* refers to an artistic arrangement of light and dark. Elders learn to look at life like this, including the shadow, and transforming it into cool, restful shade. Once darkness is accepted as good and useful, it can be distributed more agreeably.

The art of integration requires a rich palette. The bold and basic colors of youth are no longer enough. As we include more of the real world, we need more complex colors and shades, with both brilliance and depth.

It is characteristic of us elders that we accept all of ourselves as we are without question, even as we see holes we are still filling. And we are more likely to accept others as they are. We are no longer afraid of our own shadow, or those of others.

In youth we seek perfection; in elderhood, wholeness. Wholeness cannot be found in a conceptual sense, but only in reality. The integrity of age is based on embracing the whole and appreciating its unique quality. Here is the testimony of some experts in support of this view:

> *There is no light without shadow, and no psychic wholeness without imperfection.* —Carl G. Jung

> *The defects of a thing are part of the thing.* —Pierre Tielhard de Chardin

> *I am what I am 'cause I am what I am.* —Popeye the Sailor Man

. . . .

How do you combine the light and the dark in your life?

The Wisdom of Age

Successful elders reach a kind of earthy wisdom. It is not conceptual, sophisticated, or worldly-wise. We gain human wisdom, not sagacity. It is quite different from knowledge, especially theoretical knowledge from books. It is based more on practical life experience. Wisdom does not come ready-made, like some eternal truth that exists in an abstract sense, waiting to be found. You cannot find it through authority, as you might accept truth through authority. Wisdom must be handmade individually.

Wisdom is the wine made from the grapes of experience, fermented in the process of integration. The wine making is an ongoing, lifelong process. We may carry some wisdom into elderhood; we will need to build more during the years we spend there. The advantage of elders is not necessarily that we are already wise, but that we are in the best position to become wise. When we were younger we were not yet ready to make the wine of wisdom, for we were still growing the grapes of experience. Then, we could succeed at accomplishment, production, moneymaking, trendsetting, influence—but not wisdom.

Wisdom is reached through living, reflecting, and learning. A long life does not guarantee wisdom, but is necessary for it. We learn through our experience, and it takes a lot of it. Especially, it takes mistakes. In a sense, we blunder into wisdom; we do not think our way into it. We become wise by making enough mistakes, and profiting through them little by little.

· ·

At this time of life, are you growing grapes or making wine?

Part III
Becoming a Successful Elder

All old people are survivors, but not all become successful elders. Among those who do, there is great variety. Yet there are some common themes, some landmarks on the road to successful elderhood. This part presents some of these themes in terms of the strategy of successful elders, the transformation they go through, and the characteristics they achieve.

Chapter 10
Realistic Aging

Successful elders cope with both positive and negative aspects of aging in a timely and strategic way.

Topics:

Facets of Elderhood

Diversity in Age

The Downside of Age

Joy in Age

Judging Success as an Elder

Positive Aging

Strategy for Successful Elderhood

Facets of Elderhood

Elderhood has many facets. It is:

- *A stage of life*, like the stages of life that precede it, but with a different quality.
- *The successor to midlife*, not just a continuation of it. One must go through a major transition to reach elderhood, revising values and adapting life style.
- *A time for attending to life issues*, especially human issues, that may have been neglected earlier.
- *A summing up of life*, as appropriate for the last phase. It is a time of completion as a person.
- *Life climax, not anticlimax.* In terms of drama, it is the denouement, the climactic turning point upon which the play revolves, and the ending through which it finds dramatic completion—through which it is all tied together.
- *A time of continued and rapid human growth* as life draws to its climax.
- *A time of increased awareness, maturity, and depth.*
- *A time of separation, loss, and grieving,* as mates and friends die or move away, and as accustomed energy fades. Loss is an issue that must be faced and managed.
- *A preparation for death,* which succeeds it.
- *A time of maintenance* of resources that are shrinking.
- *A part of life that must be carefully planned.*

GROWTH   CLIMAX

PLANNING   STAGE OF LIFE   PREPARATION

MATURITY

SUMMING UP

Which of these facets are most important to you?

Diversity In Age

Age does not force us into a mold. Earlier in life we conform more to social patterns and pressures. Later we become more of ourselves. We have nothing to lose by being ourselves, and everything to gain. Elders explode into diversity.

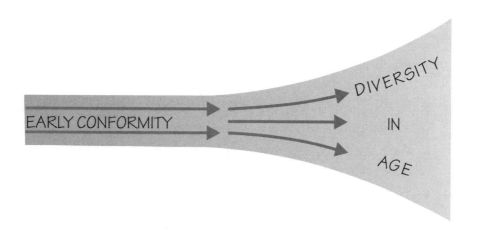

There is even greater variety among old people than in the earlier stages of life. There are old saints and old sinners, old dears and old crabs, old geniuses and old idiots, old introverts and old extroverts, old darlings and old bitches.

Developing our emerging selves with less restriction, we elders grow in unpredictable directions. Elders are ingenuous rather than fashionable. We are what we are. Conformity to style is for earlier years; elders have built their own style. Rather than seek style based on some external authority, our style emerges from within. That produces elegance. Gradually we move out of store-bought midlife into homemade elderhood.

Consider your older friends. Do you find diversity among them?
How are you yourself more of an individual than you were earlier?

The Downside of Age

Every stage of life has advantages and disadvantages. No age has exclusive advantage, but all have some. Elderhood, as well as youth and midlife, has a downside as well as an upside. Here is part of the downside that we oldsters must cope with:

♦ We are more susceptible to certain diseases. As our bodies wear and we deplete our biological allotment, the probability of disease increases. We may have to tolerate pain. Eventually, of course, we die.

♦ We have less physical energy to do the things we want to do.

♦ Finding employment may be difficult if we want to or need to be in the work force.

♦ We have to cope with loneliness if we lose our mates and long-term friends.

♦ We live in a society that has not yet discovered age. It does not know us. As our values change and grow more distant from the youth and midlife values of society, we may feel somewhat alien. Alternatively, if we accept the prevailing view of aging, we may feel superficial and desperate, lacking hope.

Elders need to recognize and deal with the downside issues of age, just as we earlier dealt with the downside of youth and midlife. But there is no advantage in dwelling on the downside here. It is already overemphasized by our culture, which tends to see nothing but downside in age. So this book emphasizes the upside of age.

. . . .
Are you more influenced by the downside of age than by its upside? Which do you think is more generally emphasized?

Joy in Age

The joy of age is in finally being who you are, in being a full, mature human, with body and mind and heart and spirit. The joy of age is finding your real self.

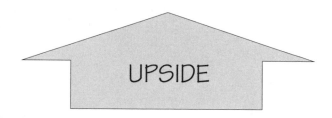

UPSIDE

Here is part of the joy that can come with successful elderhood:

♦ Elders have a *capacity to be* that is a scarce luxury in midlife. For elders, life is more likely to be a kind of celebration, less likely to be a task.

♦ Elders tend to *fit into the world* as if it belongs to us. And we cherish it.

♦ Although our time is precious, elders have a *sense of leisure*, even in the midst of activity.

♦ Out of vast experience, elders have a natural wisdom, an *innate sense of knowing*.

♦ Elders live with *wonder and appreciation* for things we earlier took for granted.

♦ Elders *live in our hearts*, a warm and juicy place to be.

♦ Reaching beyond our bodies, elders enjoy a *buoyancy of spirit*.

♦ In the achieved scope and increased depth of our lives, elders find an enriched and profound sense of *humor*.

This kind of joy is not inevitable, of course. You must work for it.

. . . .

Which of these joyful characteristics have you already experienced? Would you like more? Read on.

Judging Success as an Elder

At first we are tempted to measure ourselves in the elder years of life by the standards and values we set up in the younger years, which are also the standards and values of our culture. But the Olympic standards of youth and the performance standards of midlife are not suitable for the human and spiritual activity of elderhood. If we continue to use them, we invite failure and despair, for we are in decline in those areas.

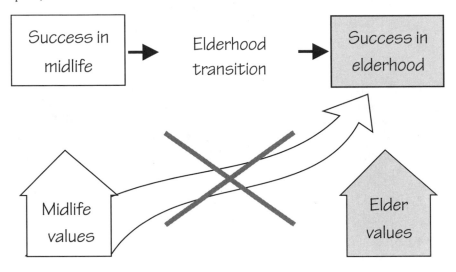

The use of youthful standards to measure mature life is foolish. The skills of age are not those requiring physical prowess and speed and productivity. We have already re-ranked our values, and those factors are no longer at top. We have discovered their inadequacy and have shifted to something more appropriate.

If we use these anachronistic standards, we do ourselves in. Life seems to be all downhill, all ending. This is a losing strategy, so we ultimately fail. To measure ourselves by our weaknesses and ignore our strengths is an unwise strategy; it does not reflect the wisdom of age.

What are suitable standards? For this pioneer age, our culture cannot suggest fitting standards; they arise from ourselves, generation after generation. Our standards should reflect our new ranking of values, with human and spiritual achievement at top.

How are you measuring your success as an elder?

Positive Aging

Positive aging is the process by which the younger person we were makes friends with the older person we are becoming.

We grow old without trying, but reaching successful elderhood requires much effort. A mature person is gradually built through many years of work.

Through positive aging we mix the callow energy of youth with the wisdom of age. We shed the energetic inexperience of youth while keeping as much of its energy as we can manage. We shed the productivity roles of midlife while keeping much of its competence.

In a sense, there is an internal battle for dominance, with our youth and midlife parts gradually weakening and shifting in importance, as our elder gradually emerges. It is not an either-or battle, but one of reconciliation. The Youth Within and the Midlifer Within are not destroyed, but rather integrated into the Full Person.

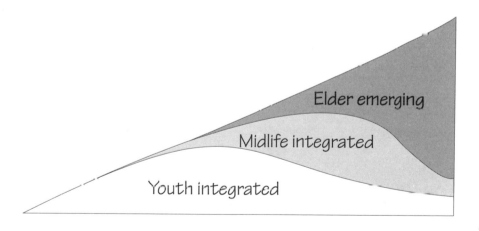

The drama of elderhood is the tug-of-war between development and decline. We win not by surviving, but by keeping on growing. A critical skill for winning is to be inner-driven and not driven by stereotypes of age.

· ·

How are the youth and midlifer within you making friends with the elder you are becoming?

Strategy for Successful Elderhood

Here are some of the most important elements in a strategy for successful elderhood:

♦ *Admit that the physical aspects of your life are going downhill,* are slowing down, are dying. You need to fight against that decline process, by enhancing wellness and lucidity as much as possible. Part of the cunning of age is knowing how to use the body wisely, to achieve more with less energy, toward the currently fitting goals.

♦ *Invest in the human and spiritual parts of life that are emergent* and becoming more available to your consciousness. Realize that these are the parts that are now most important.

♦ *Make the change to the next salient peak, the human peak.* Rerank your values accordingly, and structure your life around these new values. Let go of old value priorities that no longer serve at this stage in your life.

♦ *Measure your success in terms of your new values,* not old ones. Mobilize all your resources to achieve success in these new terms.

The incremental and decremental processes are both long and gradual. Elders need to monitor both, and be good at reconciling them.

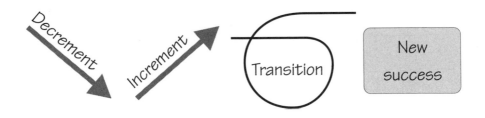

. . . .

Which elements of this strategy are most important to you at this time? What other strategies would you suggest?

Chapter 11

The Elderhood Transformation

Moving from midlife to elderhood is a major life transition. The emergence of the Full Person involves a profound change. The chief dimensions of that change are sketched in this chapter.

Topics:

Moving Beyond Ego

From Doing to Being

From Race to Ramble

From Breadth to Depth

From Single Vision to Embracing the Whole

From Head to Heart

Awareness in Age

From Rules to Guides

From Quantity to Quality

Beyond Competition to Compassion

From Physical to Spiritual Vitality

Moving Beyond Ego

In the first half of life, while we are still collecting our parts and discovering who we are, most people live in a world of ego, getting their needs met. After the full human imprint is awakened within us and the Full Person begins to emerge, we move beyond ego and become our true selves.

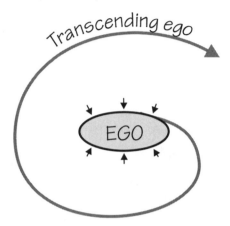

To live in ego is to organize the world around yourself, based upon needs and wants. You are at center and everything else is a projection from that center, as the Earth before Copernicus was considered the center of the universe. Your needs seem more important than those of anyone else, and they define your life and your world. There is a kind of desperate urgency about it.

Successful elders learn to transcend ego and discover the rest of their universe. It's not that their egos weaken—they are as strong as ever—but it is no longer necessary to force the world to revolve around us. We feel congruent with the world as it is. Having found our selves, we can move comfortably beyond ourselves. We inhabit the world in a new and more peaceful way. It is as if all that physical energy of the first half of life is necessary to reach escape velocity. Having escaped, we can look back and see ourselves as one bright planet among others in a large and magnificent universe. This is the birth of compassion.

This movement beyond self is also the movement into spirit.

In your own life, can you trace the journey beyond ego? What does the life of spirit mean to you?

From Doing to Being

Midlifers are *do*ers. They are goal-oriented, concerned with production, problem-solving and efficiency. They may be workaholics, an addiction considered respectable. Elders like to *be*. With fading energy, we gradually shift our emphasis from doing to being.

Unlike doing, being has no object, no goal. It just *is*, and is accepted because it is. Elders see the world and embrace it, without feeling compelled to do anything about it.

Midlife is like an urban freeway. It is built for heavy traffic and for speed. It cuts through the obstacles of the city as if they were not there. Elderhood is like a winding rural byway. There is less traffic, and driving is more pleasant. One can enjoy the countryside while passing through. The road flows through the terrain gracefully, but it is not built for high speed.

In age our attention shifts from the destination to the journey. *Getting there* is no longer at the center of our lives. In a sense, we feel that we have already gotten there. We have arrived. We want to enjoy *being here*. Successful elders gradually move from work identity to self identity. In aging we gradually get out of the fast lane, slow down, turn off the freeway and head for the byway.

How much of your life is engaged in doing, and how much in being?

From Race to Ramble

In elderhood we rediscover the neglected poetry of our lives. In his well-known sonnet, Wordsworth voices the midlife complaint:

> The world is too much with us. Late and soon,
> Getting and spending, we lay waste our powers.
> Little we see in nature that is ours.

Elders break free of the pressing demands of midlife and wake up to the world around us. Finally, we can smell the roses without picking them.

This does not mean that elders become idle. We may be quite active, but our lives are no longer centered on production, so our activity is not frenetic and anxious. A sense of leisure or playfulness begins to permeate our lives and even our work.

In the sense of Robert Frost, a more mature poet: Even though we elders have miles to go before we sleep, we still, in the midst of our winter evening, stop by woods and watch them fill up with snow. Why this leisurely attitude, even though we have promises to keep? Simply because the woods are lovely, dark, and deep, and we are connected to all these qualities.

We work free of the rat race and approach life deliberately but easily, with more appreciation and more leisure to follow wherever it leads. Life becomes a journey filled less with activity and more with awareness. It is filled less with duty and more with joyful acceptance. It is less of a chore and more of an adventure.

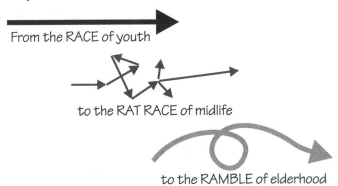

From the RACE of youth

to the RAT RACE of midlife

to the RAMBLE of elderhood

Are you in a race or on a ramble? How do you want to be?

From Breadth to Depth

In youth we "grow up." In adulthood we tend to "grow out," to expand, to grow sideways (we are not speaking only of "middle-age spread"). We add stability, structure, coherence. In elderhood we tend to "grow down." We add depth, individuality, soul.

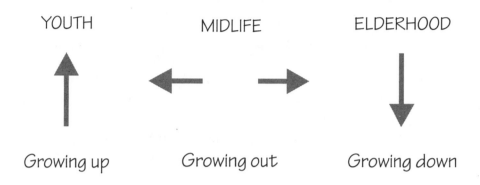

YOUTH   MIDLIFE   ELDERHOOD

Growing up   Growing out   Growing down

In the first half of life, we are expanding our agenda, and are likely to see it in physical or economic terms. We are collectors. In the second half, we are working on what we have already col lected, contracting it and integrating it. We are building a unified whole out of all those parts. This is difficult work. And we want satisfying results; oversimplifications will not do.

Each phase of life is preparation for the next, so all of life is preparation for elderhood—for a life of human depth. Later preparation is not formal, like earlier education, and the activity we are preparing for is not aimed at making money, so we may at first be tempted to discount it. Gradually we come to realize that all of our earlier education and experience has prepared us for what we are now becoming.

Depth fits with elderhood. If we realize this and accept the challenge of seeking depth, our lives have a sense of fitting profundity, whatever our accomplishments. If we do not, our lives seem unsuitably shallow in the absence of the depth that age calls for.

· ·

At this time of life, are you growing up, out, or down?

From Single Vision to Embracing the Whole

Midlife is expansionistic; it wants to acquire more elements. Elderhood is holistic; it wants to embrace the whole. The logic of midlife has the concentrated focus of an arrow on the bullseye. The perception of age includes the full target and the surrounding terrain. Midlife is focused, exclusive, and businesslike in its doing and producing. Elderhood is broad, inclusive, and diffuse. It is attentive but relaxed in its being and living.

The human eye has an angle of visual acuity of only about four degrees. To see beyond that with precision, we must keep repositioning the narrow center of attention. The eye has an angle of peripheral vision of almost 180 degrees, in which it perceives the whole picture in a more diffuse way. We need both functions to get along. Midlife is like the busily scanning center of vision; elderhood is like the relaxed but attentive peripheral vision.

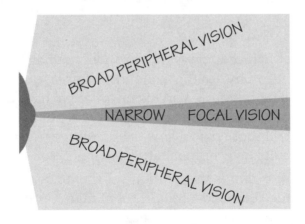

Elders think in terms of wholes. Their thrust is to unite; every part of the whole relates to the rest of it. That is the attitude of integration. It no longer seems urgent to define all the parts and put them together like a jigsaw puzzle. It seems more important to appreciate the whole and be grateful for it.

We can still focus on the parts and be analytical, for we learned how to do that well. But we are reluctant to put on analytical blinders for fear of missing the whole. Age is a time for discovering and appreciating unity.

· ·

How much are you using the "peripheral vision" of age?

From Head to Heart

All of us, especially men, are taught the value of thought; feeling is not as much valued. We are encouraged to live in our heads. As we age and go from breadth to depth, our center of knowing tends to move from our heads down to our hearts. We do not reject the head, but we no longer give it exclusive billing.

Throughout midlife we listened carefully to the words; in elderhood we are ready to listen to the music. The heart becomes the well of all thought. We are less eager to analyze things; we would rather appreciate them.

We gradually let go of the need to understand and control everything. That seemed appropriate earlier; now it seems confining. In a sense, we transcend understanding and go directly to knowing. A religious widow of 84 put it this way:

"When I was younger, I thought that life should be the way I liked it to be, and I was crushed when it wasn't. Now I'm more accepting. I may not understand God's purposes in my life, but I just trust Him."

When we no longer need to control the world, our minds work differently. We do not have to analyze, argue, and defend. We do not have to exhaustively examine the detailed parts of that which we grasp more directly. Gradually, we become less driven by pure thought and more driven by feeling. We move toward appreciation, wonder, awe, and mystery. The poetry of age emerges.

This shift is most prominent in men, who have neglected heart more. It is less apparent in women, who are more likely to be living in their hearts already, and who recently have more cultural opportunity to move in the opposite direction.

. . . .

How much are you head-centered? Heart-centered? Toward which are you moving?

Awareness in Age

As we age we become more aware of the world around us. The doors of perception slowly swing open on the hinges of age.

People become more real. Earlier in life we are likely to see other persons in terms of their roles: mother, husband, possible mate, boss, and so forth. In age we are more likely to look through the role and see the person. Animals, plants, and even lifeless minerals also become more real. We let them be what they are, and our being has a kind of creature-to-creature dialogue with theirs.

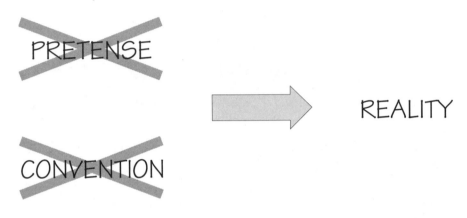

Earlier in ego-centered life we are likely to see what we need to see. In elderhood we are more likely to see what is there. We let in the essential nature of the persons and things we observe. What have we got to lose? With a sense of contemplation, we become *realizers;* we see with openness and wonder. We relate more totally to things in a kind of cosmic embrace. In the words of a man in his 60s, suffering from serious cancer: "I have always loved roses, but I have never *seen* them like this before."

The awareness of elders is a mystical and spiritual perception. We let it all in, not because we can use it or make a profit on it; we let it in as a gift. Then we are full of wonder and gratitude.

Seeing more is normal in age, but not automatic. It requires cooperation, practice, and stretching. If we do not stretch in this way, we shrink. Oldsters become either more sensitive or less.

. . . .

Can you realize *a tree as well as see it? For you, what is the difference?*

From Rules to Guides

In age we no longer run our lives by following rigid rules. Relying on our depth of experience, we find that general guides are enough. Where earlier we saw requirements, in elderhood we see possibilities.

We are taught to anticipate aging as a process of shrinking. Surprisingly, it turns out to be in some respects a spreading out from the narrower focus of earlier life, a diffusing, a broadening, an opening of possibilities in a larger, more human world. Although there are still more than enough externally imposed requirements, the trend with age is from system-imposed rules that are followed out of duty to more general, self-imposed guides that are followed in the spirit of exploration and adventure.

Not driven by as many conventional rules, elders choose which of many possibilities to turn into realities. We ask, "What is essential for me? What do I really want?" This requires self-discipline, choice, management, and adherence to core values.

Do you run your life more by fixed rules or flexible guides?

From Quantity to Quality

Earlier in life, we pursue wealth in terms of quantity and money. In elderhood, when human values have priority, wealth takes on a new meaning. The value we place on money and acquisition shrinks as we realize the truth in the statement, "You can't take it with you."

We are no longer content to spend our shrinking time and energy on acquisition, or on preparing for a life that comes later. We want to live *now*. Quantity is running out; quality has been neglected. In earlier years we might have been willing to sacrifice much quality of life in the frantic pursuit of wealth. Now we want vintage living, quality choices. The highest thing in life is quality experience.

We become experts at quality, connoisseurs filling our precious days with the best quality of life that we can manage. We decide for ourselves what quality means. It may be scarcely recognized by conventional midlife standards, and it is usually not what the world wants to sell us. We want quality as measured by our new human standards, as we ourselves define them. It need not be expensive, but it must be real.

Earlier we were willing to pursue happiness; now we want to possess joy. The change is profound. Earlier, with ample time before us, the pursuit was enough. Like playing the lottery, it was based on the hope of good fortune in the future. Now we want possession today. We want true joy.

What do you do with happiness? You pursue it.
What do you do with joy? You possess it.

How do you manage your "quality control" for the quality of your life?

Beyond Competition to Compassion

In age, we want to reach beyond the win-lose paradigm of competition to find a win-win paradigm that fits better for our human work. Competitive gaming is divisive. One must defend some and oppose others, and sit on one side or the other of the fence. We elders, with our holistic viewpoint and our drive toward unity, appreciate both sides of the fence, and find cooperation more satisfying than competition.

WIN-LOSE   WIN-WIN

Empathy and compassion fill the gap left as competition shrinks. Elders are empathic because we have already walked a mile in the other's moccasins. We are compassionate because we have suffered the other's pain.

Compassion comes from the work of integrating a lifetime of experience. We elders have been there. As we watch the show in the Theater of Life, we see ourselves in each of the characters, and play the role with them. We are Everywoman and Everyman.

Best of all, our compassion extends even to ourselves. We accept ourselves as we are, blemishes and all.

. . . .

What are some things that earlier you would have judged harshly but now you accept with compassion?

From Physical to Spiritual Vitality

The vitality of youth bubbles out of wild, untamed physical energy. The vitality of midlife oozes out of a disciplined, productive energy, faithful even if depleted. *The vitality of elderhood radiates from a pervasive spiritual energy.*

Young vigor is orgasmic, muscular, pushing, making it, physical. It is a quantitative thrust to make life happen. Elder vigor is rooted in values and beliefs. It is a qualitative thrust to appreciate and embrace life.

Young vigor is acquisitive, centripetal, pulling material things towards itself. Elder vigor is giving, radiant, centrifugal, reaching beyond self into spirit.

Two complementary tasks of aging are:

♦ to husband and hold on to the physical vitality of youth as much as reasonable, and

♦ to foster the growth of the spiritual vitality of age as much as possible.

Where are you in the shift from the physical to the spiritual?

Chapter 12

Ten Marks of Successful Elders

How can you spot a successful elder—one who has avoided the cultural pitfalls, navigated the elderhood transition, and arrived at true elderhood? Such a person will be living and enjoying the qualities of age as much as his or her handicaps and resources permit, and it will show.

There are no fixed standards in the pioneer territory of elderhood. Even if there were, we elders are such a diverse and independent group that we would rearrange them to suit ourselves. Yet there are some common qualities that we intuitively sense and admire in those who have embraced elderhood and found the special joy that it offers. These qualities are the marks of successful elders. They are some of the gems inside the geode of age.

Mark 1. Elders See Time as Life

Mark 2. Elder Have Presence

Mark 3. Elders Stay Engaged in Living

Mark 4. Elders Have Mature Adaptability

Mark 5. Elders Are Free

Mark 6. Elders Are Candid

Mark 7. Elders Are Generalists

Mark 8. Elders Seek Essence

Mark 9. Elders Find Peace

Mark 10. Elders Find Cosmic Humor

Mark 1. Elders See Time as Life

To successful elders, time is a precious gift. Our response to this gift is appreciation and reverence for life. What was commonplace in earlier years—a walk in a garden, a sunset, a talk with a friend—is imbued with wonder and magic. We want to fill our days with this appreciation of the commonplace as wonderful.

Eldertime is "on loan." We see it as more life, more opportunity, more daily adventure, more beauty, more human connection. "I have only today," says a woman in her eighties. "I may be gone tomorrow." It is a matter-of-fact statement, said not with fear for tomorrow's absence, but with appreciation and joy for today's precious presence.

In midlife, time is money. In age, time is life.

There is a paradox in elders' view of time. Time is running out, yet there is no rush. Wrapped in the essence of life, and pursuing only values of highest priority, elders proceed with a sense of leisure. The midlifer is a begrudging engineer of passing time; the elder is a generous user of borrowed time. The midlifer faces deadlines and turns to work; the elder faces death and turns to life. That life is no longer a substance to be divided and manipulated; it is a totality to be revered.

. . . .

How much of your time has become eldertime?

Mark 2. Elders Have Presence

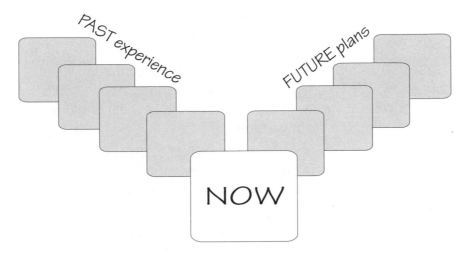

Their view of time gives elders a striking presence. As the quantity of remaining time shrinks, the quality of time seems to be squeezed out of the past and future and into the present.

Much of our lives we live elsewhere: in the past, in the future, in our thoughts. Successful elders live in the here-and-now, with awareness, moment by moment. We discover, finally, that all the world is in each single instant.

In age life is a day-by-day adventure. We are more likely to take it as it comes, to flow with it, to be in the moment. Our goal shifts from future success to present vitality. We are less willing to mortgage today to earn for tomorrow. We are less willing to deal in abstraction with reality so close by. We are less willing to be in our heads without the company of our hearts.

There is a mental, psychological, and spiritual transformation through which elders gain this presence. If we are successful, we live in a new and more profound way. We can admire a tree or a flower and seem to be embracing and appreciating the whole world in this simple act.

Said one man in his seventies: "It's as if I have been looking at life all these years as a stack of snapshots, and have now discovered that it's a movie."

How much of your life is in the here-and-now?

Mark 3. Elders Stay Engaged in Living

Successful elders are fully engaged in living. Our activity may change with age, but our engagement goes on. The change is like that on an old-style telephone plugboard, when the operator disconnects one cord and plugs in another. We get connected to something new. We successful elders tend our plugboards—when we lose the connection with old interests, old friends, or old activities, we plug in new connections.

Society invites us to disengage, saying: "You're finished with the important part of life. Go out to pasture." Successful elders know this is poor advice. Our activity in age needs to use everything we have—mind, body, and spirit.

Society says, "Go from work to leisure," where leisure means withdrawal and play. For the successful elder, leisure is rather a peaceful state of mind and absence of distraction—an environment in which we find more opportunity for new engagement.

Elders are advised, "Keep busy." This can be misleading advice. Successful elders do not seek activity just for the sake of being busy. Busy work is even less appropriate than earlier because elders are living on borrowed time and do not want to spend it on anything that is not important to them. Better advice is, "Keep engaged with what fascinates you and pursues your cutting edge."

To be engaged in life does not mean to keep doing what we were doing earlier. Some of the activity of earlier life is no longer available or appropriate, but a new world of opportunities is always there. In elderhood, activity flows from essence. What we do flows from who we are. Having followed the advice of Socrates, *Know thyself*, we move on to its natural consequence, *Be thyself*.

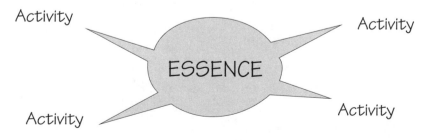

How do you stay engaged in meaningful activity?

Mark 4. Elders Have Mature Adaptability

Life changes radically from midlife to elderhood, then keeps on changing in elderhood. We successful elders keep remodeling our past lives to serve us better as times change.

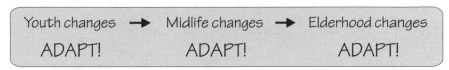

There is a paradox and a challenge in the flexibility of elders. As our bodies are becoming less resilient, our minds and spirits are called upon to be more resilient. Our world is broader and richer, and we must adapt to it with integrity, without oversimplifying. There is a trend through the second half of life from conceptual rigidity to a more realistic and organic adaptability.

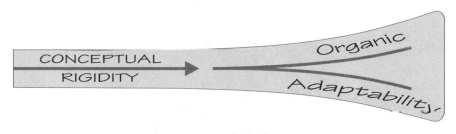

Adaptation in elders is not simple compliance. It does not mean to flow like water downhill, or to accept passively whatever comes along. We elders are not putty to be shaped by others, for we are already strong individuals. We adapt by finding suitable ways to express our strong individuality within that part of our environment we cannot change. We cling to our central values and beliefs, but express them in forms that are currently available.

We practice what Albert Schweitzer called positive resignation—the deliberate and wholehearted acceptance of the best choices available to us.

A good guide for mature adaptability is Reinhold Niebuhr's Serenity Prayer, used by Alcoholics Anonymous and others:

God grant me the serenity to accept the things I cannot change, the courage to change the things I can, and the wisdom to know the difference.

. . . .

How can you use this prayer to guide your adaptation?

Mark 5. Elders Are Free

Many midlifers dream of breaking free of regimented life and becoming more self-driven. Elders finally do break free. Life is not as pressing and not as structured. There are fewer external demands and constraints. We are captains in charge of our own ships, sailing where we will, not bound by fixed course and schedule.

We lighten up as we get older. We get rid of our mortgages—not only the money we owe to the bank for our houses, but also the burdens that mortgaged our lives. We can move on to all the living that we put on hold.

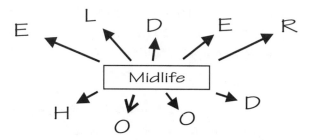

This is a mixed blessing, for we find that it takes a lot of discipline to manage our newfound freedom. We need to learn to guide our daily routine in a new way, and this requires new skills. With fewer external rules, we need to learn to live by our own internal guides. Like men who leave structured corporate jobs to start their own businesses, we become entrepreneurs of our own lives. We learn to set our own priorities and schedules, and to manage our lives in pursuit of our new values.

If we do this successfully, life becomes more like a dance; we flow with it. Free of rigid structure, we find joy in the process of daily living. Free of pretense, we find joy in reality. Free of the imposed goals of others, we find joy in being ourselves. Free of the need to acquire possessions, we seize and enjoy what we already have—what we are.

In our search for spirit, we anticipate breaking free even from our bodies.

. . . .
Are you gradually breaking free as you age? Can you manage your new freedom?

Mark 6. Elders Are Candid

It is a natural, innate gift of age to be clear, frank, and direct about things we care for. We elders know our values and follow them. When younger, we might negotiate, tentatively testing to see if our viewpoint is popular and safe. In age, we say what we think. We sense there is nothing to lose, and no time to waste.

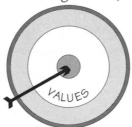

Elders have a compelling lucidity and powerful spiritual energy in pursuing what we value. Unfettered from the shackles of midlife, operating out of integrity, and anchored in a sense of meaning that is greater than ourselves, we simply and directly follow our top values wherever they lead. We want to embed those values in the world while we are able. When younger we worried about the image we were projecting to others, and were tempted to embellish that image with pretense. Successful elders move beyond pretense. We say, in effect, "Here I am. This is me. What you see is what you get." Instead of wanting to be who we were, or pretending to be who we are not, we allow ourselves to be who we are.

We transcend the need to deny. On the physical level, we gradually befriend our bodies as they are and no longer try to hide the gray or put on a shell of youth.

Earlier in life we learned to be indirect and devious, like politicians hedging and saying the expected thing, trying to please everyone. Now we are more straightforward, ingenuous, perhaps even blunt. As we become better integrated, we tend to become persons of few words. We are truth-sayers.

We develop congruence, the art of being ourselves. What we do and what we say flows out of who we are and fits for us. So it comes out straight and clear.

How are you following your values more directly as you age?

Mark 7. Elders Are Generalists

In a world that favors specialization, elders are generalists. Although we are individually unique, we belong to the whole more than to any part. Our thinking is in terms of unity rather than analysis. Our thrust is toward integration rather than partitioning.

As we move beyond ego, our concern gradually grows to include not just personal values, but those of the family; not just family values, but those of the community; not just community values, but those of the culture. Finally, we embrace the values of all humanity.

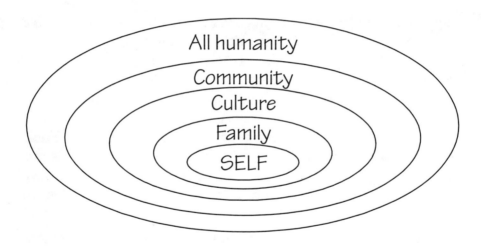

Elders are equipped by our state of human development to be statespersons of integration and bridge-builders in our fragmented society.

. . . .

Where are you in the process of becoming a generalist?

Mark 8. Elders Seek Essence

As we become rich, individual, integrated persons, we need to express who we are becoming. We seek and express our essence. We express it in words and in action, but especially in being—we are who we are.

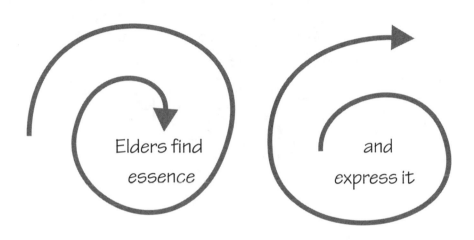

Elders find essence   and express it

Elders seek simple, uncluttered lives by sweeping out, as much as practicable, whatever is nonessential, alien, or system-imposed, thus making more space for their essence. Elder asks two questions: *Is it truly me?* and *For me, is it truly important?*

Whatever passes these two tests, however simple, is washed in significance.

How are you expressing your essential self as you age?

Mark 9. Elders Find Peace

Full of experience, past the midlife grind, discovering and expressing who we are, and getting to the essence, elders feel a sense of contentment. We achieve a peace that was not possible earlier in life, even if we were successful by midlife standards.

The world is our friend rather than our enemy. We no longer fight against it. We cherish it, despite its shortcomings. We live in it, and are comfortable with it. There is a wonderful feeling of spreading out, of occupying and living in the whole world, rather than in a narrower space, as seemed necessary earlier. We no longer try to explain our world; we simply know it and embrace it.

There is a sense of having enough, at least in the human realm. There is a sense of unity, of oneness, of connection with the world at a deep level. We no longer need to be busily pursuing fortune and happiness, for we have found joy.

Youth wants the bubbles in the spa, and surrounds itself with their noise and turbulence. Elderhood enjoys the calm, warm, caressing water. Without the turbulence we can enjoy the peace, see the reflections on the surface of the water, watch the world and enjoy it.

Elders are more peaceful more of the time. For us it is a natural state, and it is very satisfying. We do not have to go to Las Vegas, Paris, or Timbuktu to get a fix.

. . . .

Have you moved from asking Where did I go wrong? *to asking* Where did I go right? *to simply and peacefully reviewing* Where did I go?

Mark 10. Elders Find Cosmic Humor

There is fullness of humor that arrives with age, a bittersweet humor of life lived. Since we have cried more, we can laugh more.

Elders alive today have lived through decades when negative, blaming, put-down humor was in vogue. We doubtless laughed at it at the time, and used it ourselves, but no longer. We have built too much compassion for others to make a joke of putting them down.

If anyone is the butt of elder humor, it is ourselves. In a sense, life seems like a joke told by God, and it's on us. But it's on everyone else also, and it's not a put-down.

Looking back in age at the cosmic tragicomedy of life, some of it demands tears and some of it invites laughter, and for much of it either tears or laughter is appropriate. Given our choice, it is preferable to laugh, like the old Chinese sage of Happiness. Laughter shakes and jostles our physical parts and also our spiritual parts. If those parts have become strained and deformed by the pressures and stresses of life, the laughter of age urges them back into more natural and comfortable relationship. Laughter is a spiritual breakthrough that transcends the mundane.

As we draw the circle of life wider, we include more things to laugh about. As we integrate the things within our circle, we want our humor to reflect our integration. We want even our humor to mirror essence. We love the fantasy and the sense of incongruity that is at the heart of humor, and we want it to resonate with life as we are coming to know it.

Elders are serious, but not sober and heavy. Wisdom wears a smile, and humor is close to spirit.

Have a joyous elderhood!

Part IV
Making the Most of Your Elder Years

The years of elderhood are pioneer territory. They require a new approach and new skills. Our bodies are in gradual decline, and that decline must be managed. Our spirits are emerging, and must be encouraged and nourished.

Elderhood is, in a sense, bracketed by death—an unpopular but unavoidable topic. We must deal with the distant approach of death as we enter elderhood, and finally meet death as we leave. Here we consider death to put it in its proper place, to prevent it from interfering with life, and to use it to enrich elderhood. The nearness of death can give birth to new levels of life.

Chapter 13
The Key to Elderhood

By idolizing youth and fearing death, we are prepared for despair and depression. We are given little hope of power and potency in age. We are not taught to deal with death and to value age. We must discover these things ourselves, for through them we reclaim power and control.

The key for entering elderhood is accepting the approach of death and coming to terms with it. This needs to be done long before death is immanent. Until we come to terms with death, it hangs over the remainder of life like a cloud blocking the sun.

Topics:

> Reactions to the Approach of Death
> Can There Be Joy While Approaching Death?
> Making a Friend of Death
> Fear of Death
> Ways of Coping with the Approach of Death

Reactions to the Approach of Death

Age brings the realization that there are relatively few years left (even though it may turn out to be decades). Here are some common attitudes stirred up by the approach of death:

- ◆ "Eat, drink, and be merry, for at dawn we die."
- ◆ My life is finished.
- ◆ It is time to bring my life to completion.
- ◆ It's a pity I messed up my life, but it's too late now.
- ◆ If life ends in death, it is a waste.
- ◆ Time is precious, and I will live as fully as I can.
- ◆ If I die today, it will have been a good and full life.
- ◆ I better get my affairs in order.
- ◆ What will I leave behind as my gift to posterity?
- ◆ I worked hard; it's time to have fun.
- ◆ If I'm not going to be around, what's the difference?
- ◆ I'd better finish the job.
- ◆ There's not much time, so why bother with the remaining years?
- ◆ The remaining years are very precious because they are few.
- ◆ I have no time to waste on anything except what is essential and truly important.
- ◆ How can I be creative about the way I live the rest of my life?

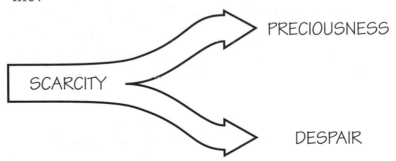

Which of these attitudes fit for you? Which do you think most appropriate?

Can There Be Joy While Approaching Death?

In every phase of life we are, of course, approaching closer to death. In earlier phases, however, it is remote enough that we can ignore it or postpone consideration of it. So we can look forward to the next stage. In youth we look forward to adulthood and midlife. In midlife we look forward to elderhood. Elderhood is the last stage of life. What we have to look forward to is death—the end of life as we know it.

For any age, honesty in aging is acceptance of where we are in the present stage, and acceptance of what comes next. There is joy in youth, and the honest youth enjoys it knowing that he or she will become a midlifer. There is joy in midlife, and the honest midlifer enjoys it knowing that he or she will become an elder. There is joy in elderhood, and the honest elder enjoys it knowing that he or she will die.

There is joy in beginning a piece of work, a different joy in working through the details, and a still different joy in bringing it to completion. The joy that comes into life in elderhood has a special quality and intensity *because* death is closer. Finally, our work of art is coming to completion.

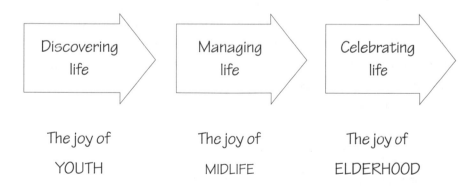

Discovering life → Managing life → Celebrating life

The joy of YOUTH   The joy of MIDLIFE   The joy of ELDERHOOD

Which kind of joy do you prefer, or are you willing to rotate through all three?

Making a Friend of Death

Death does not change as we age, but we become more aware of it, and use its approach to design our lives. Typically, our view of death changes like this:

> Until 30s: *"I won't die—old people die."*
> 40s: *"Maybe I'll die someday."*
> 50s: *"Someday I'm going to die."*
> 60s: *"I must come to terms with death."*
> 70s: *"I must be ready for death."*
> 80s: *"I am ready for death when it comes."*

Death is a distant concept to youngsters. They are only beginning to live, and have not yet arrived at many of the basic benchmarks of life. The idea of being close to death is unacceptable, unthinkable, and fills them with a fear of impotence and a fear of missing out on life. Many young people find that old people present an unwelcome clue of death, so they edit them out of life; they may not even see them.

To elders, death becomes a palpable reality as we suffer the death of many friends and feel the hot breath of our own death ever closer.

To youth, death is an evil, irreconcilable, unmanageable enemy, much as the Soviet Union was to the Western world for years. It is a concept seen in black-and-white stills. With age there comes an acceptance, a reconciliation, a realization that the approach of death brings quality into life. Gradually, age makes a friend of death.

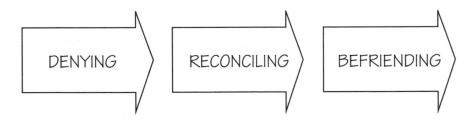

DENYING ⟩ RECONCILING ⟩ BEFRIENDING ⟩

Where are you in the process of befriending death?

Fear of Death

Everyone fears death to some extent. Some good reasons for fearing it are:

♦ *It is a profound loss.* All of our experience and our philosophy are built around life as we know it, yet we are forced to let it go. Life is about being and becoming, but death is ostensibly a gateway to non-being.

♦ *It is unknown.* Death cannot be known until we reach it. Other stages of life can be foreknown through the testimony of those who have reached them. Death cannot, for those who reach it never report back in the normal manner. Religions give us sketches of an afterlife, but they are vague concepts that must be accepted on faith, and are still unknown.

♦ *Dying involves pain.* Even if we feel finished with life and are ready to let go, we will probably want to avoid or minimize the pain involved in the process.

Youth fears death; for youth, death is distant and horrid, and seems avoidable. As we age, life seems more complete and death more natural. The fear may diminish, but not go away. Death is still a loss; it is still unknown. Dying is still painful, and the pain may already be with us. Yet if we are successful elders, we will be reasonably ready when it comes.

. . . .

What is your level of fear of death? Is it manageable? What is your level of preparation? Will you be ready?

Ways of Coping with the Approach of Death

There are four ways that we deal with the approach of death:

◆ *Ignore it.* This can be done in youth, but not thereafter.

◆ *Deny it and try to hide it.* The heavy load of the decline view causes many to try this approach. It is easy in youth, but becomes increasingly untenable as we age. It takes serious denial not to accept eventual death when one reaches old age.

◆ *Dwell on it and be absorbed by it.* The failure of the earlier approaches leads many to this dismal one.

◆ *Accept it and prepare for it.* The human view of life as ongoing development invites this approach.

If we deny death we may be haunted by it. If we dwell on death needlessly we may be depressed by it.

Death does not hide well; there are too many reminders of it. Death will not be denied; attempting to do so reveals it with renewed strength. Accepting it as a normal part of life and preparing for it is the only winning strategy. If we do that, death recedes into its natural place, and we can get on with living.

To sail into elderhood, we must navigate the narrow strait between denial and depression. On the maps our culture provides, this is poorly charted territory.

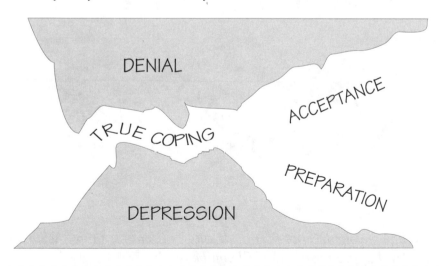

DENIAL

ACCEPTANCE

TRUE COPING

PREPARATION

DEPRESSION

In which of these ways are you coping with the approach of death?

Chapter 14

Managing Decline

We learn to manage incline but not decline. We learn to manage our lives in the early years when everything is growing. We become skilled at handling beginnings and only later discover, to our surprise, that we must also handle endings. Elders are like business executives who learned their management skills in times of heady economic expansion and now face the task of downsizing. Like those executives, elders must learn to do more with less.

Physical decline is the context in which the human growth of elders takes place. Although it is not the central focus, it is an important part of the territory, and elders need to know how to manage it. This chapter suggests some guidelines.

Topics:

Both Growth and Decline

The Fortunes and Handicaps of Age

Management of Resources

The Soft Law of Decline

The Myth of Debility

Guide 1: *Cherish Your Body*

Guide 2: *Stretch and Learn*

Guide 3: *Let Go*

The Losses of Elderhood

Guide 4: *Adapt*

Accepting Physical Loss

Elder Energy Budget.

Both Growth and Decline

Every living thing experiences both growth and decline. Some element of progressive loss followed by death is found in every organism and every artifact. The decline view of aging is natural, but it must be counterbalanced by a principle of growth.

Growth and development throughout life is natural and necessary. Every organism follows a process of unfolding its essence, expressing its inner nature. This is not a simple, linear process. One aspect comes into prominence, then fades as another comes to the fore. Life flows with a cyclical rhythm, fostering the emergence of essential nature from birth to death.

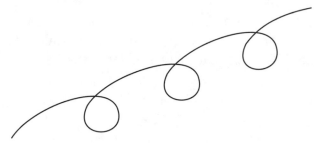

Living things establish a dynamic balance between growth and decline. This balancing act is especially important in elderhood. The physical part of life is like a promontory jutting out to sea, which becomes narrower and steeper as we go along. As we proceed along this promontory, we feel the need to complete our development. Also, we feel a hunger to transcend—to reach beyond ourselves. Life becomes a cosmic tug-of-war between our physical entropy and our spiritual yearning.

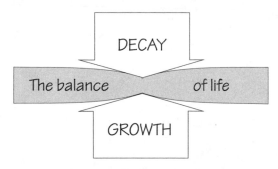

What balance are you striking between growth and decline at this time?

The Fortunes and Handicaps of Age

Life is neither ideal nor fair. By some cosmic accidents, we start out with different genetic machinery, different parents, family, and community, and different economic and cultural environments. That establishes our starting conditions, and we take it from there. No conditions are perfect, though some seem better than others. We all have, so to speak, a starting handicap.

We can control some aspects of our lives but not others. If my draw in the genetic lottery includes a fatal weakness, or I have an accident, or inherit a fortune, or lose one, or get cancer, my handicap changes suddenly. Otherwise it changes slowly as I wear out.

Our handicaps do not change the basic thrust of human life; they establish constraints. A man who is paralyzed by a stroke in his 50s still has the task of planning and living his elderhood, though he is now physically constrained. His outlook is not as good unless he compensates. Some people use severe handicaps as prods to live at a higher level; for example, Franklin D. Roosevelt and Helen Keller.

Our physical handicaps are likely to worsen slowly. Gradually, we become unable to do some things we could do earlier. Successfully aging persons realize this, and are not undone by the loss of behavior taken for granted when younger. They keep on going. They look at what is left and make it work for what they want to do with the rest of their lives.

Many worry about losing their mental ability, but most experience only a gradual slowing and a change of style, often an improvement. Throughout life we shift into new modalities of thinking as needed. Some mental styles are fitting in youth, others are fitting in elderhood. Most of us use only a small portion of our mental capacity, and have more than enough brain function to accommodate changes as they are needed.

. . . .

What handicap are you operating under at this time? If it changes, for better or worse, can you still go on?

Management of Resources

As noted, the physical aspect is the base on which we build our human life, and the economic aspect is a supporting buttress. These two aspects, though not the essence of life, are major resources. We need to maintain a physical base that is adequate to build on. Eventually this base crumbles and life becomes insupportable. By physical management we hope to delay the crumbling until it is inevitable. By economic management we hope to keep some supporting buttresses in place as long as we need them. The reason for managing either our physical base or our economic support is to allow human growth to go on.

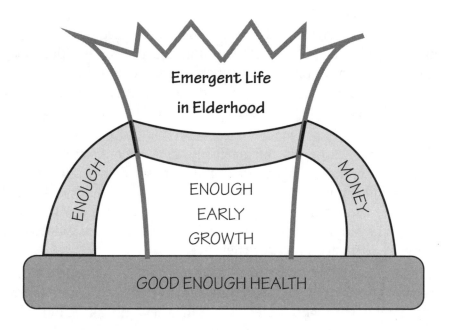

The management task in elderhood is the same as in other phases of life. The task is to live as we want to live and do what we want to do in the context of limited resources. Some of our resources are ample, some are scarce—that is our handicap. Whatever that handicap is, and however it changes, the objective remains the same.

. . . .

What are the resources that you need to manage in order to have a full human life in elderhood? Which are ample? Which are scarce? Can you manage?

The Soft Law of Decline

It is true that our bodies are declining, but it is also true that they have amazing powers of recovery and survival. For the most part, our bodies are good friends; they are flexible and they are experts at survival. We can thank them for having carried us all this distance through life, and trust that they will keep on doing a good job for us.

Decline is a fact, but it is a soft fact. As a long term trend, it is inexorable. The short term trend, however, is more manageable. It can be up or down. In elderhood, as in any other stage of life, we will experience both.

Over the long run, we know that our bodies will slow down, and will eventually disintegrate in death. Over the shorter run they can serve us well, and may even improve. Some elders enjoy better health throughout elderhood than they did in abusive midlife.

There is a great deal of difference between the physical decline that the culture expects and the good health and vitality that is possible for most elders. As individuals we can be anywhere in between the vigorous health that is possible and the debility that is expected, and we have some control, though not full control, of where.

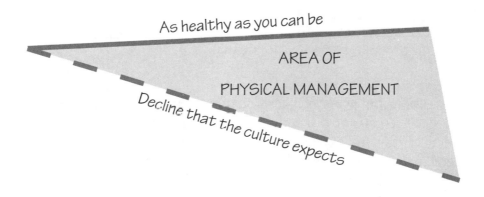

As healthy as you can be

AREA OF

PHYSICAL MANAGEMENT

Decline that the culture expects

What is the pattern of your own physical decline? Were there any sudden drops? Is any part better than it used to be? Do you have good enough health to enjoy human fullness?

The Myth of Debility

There is a myth, created in a world of youngsters, that many of the parts of a person die as the person ages, so that in elderhood little is left but a shell. One example is the assumption, that can be made at almost any age, that persons 20 or 30 years older do not or cannot make love. Another is the unthinking assumption that a person of eightysomething does not or cannot feel passion. It would be a more reasonable assumption that the octogenarian must be passionate to have supported life to that age.

A person of 30 is likely to think of a person of 70 as out to pasture in Vegetableland. Yet when the thirtysomething grows to be seventysomething and still feels vital, sexy, and passionate, he is likely to revise his ideas about age. Of course he has forty years to do so, and the change is gradual.

There is no reason one cannot be sexual in the 70s, 80s, or 90s. The soft rule of decline applies, of course. Passion may not burn with as much blinding heat as in the past, yet it builds a pervasive intensity. It is an abiding and peaceful intensity. There is no longer the need to prove virility that is felt in earlier years.

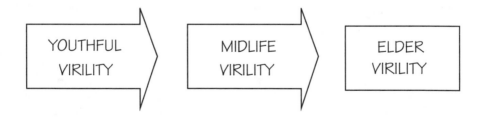

Passion changes with age; it changes between adolescence and 30, between 30 and 60, and between 60 and 90. There is likely to be more raw and explosive energy in the sexuality of the adolescent; more depth, warmth, and intimacy in the sexuality of the elder; and that of the midlifer is likely to be somewhere in between.

One can be sexual at 70. Or 80. Or 90.

. . . .

How do you deal with the myth of debility? Are you discovering more intensity and virility in age than you expected?

Guide 1: *Cherish Your Body*

In the next few pages are some general guides that are helpful to elders in managing their bodies in the context of decline. The first guide is: *Cherish your body.*

As our bodies wear, they require more maintenance and care. They become less tolerant of abuse, and complain more when it occurs. Youth thinks the body will take enormous abuse, and gets away with it for some time. Age reveals the limits of the body and also its power. Youth tends to take the body for granted; age necessarily gets to know it better, to discover its idiosyncrasies, to respect it, and to cherish it.

As our bodies weaken, we may at first feel deserted, betrayed and angry that they will not serve us as before. Eventually, we become reconciled. We listen to them more and abuse them less. Our physical limitations make our bodies somehow more real and even more lovable.

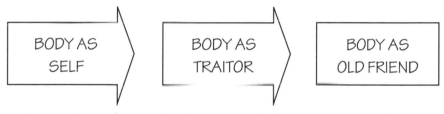

BODY AS SELF → BODY AS TRAITOR → BODY AS OLD FRIEND

In youth we *are* our bodies; in midlife we overdrive them; in age we grow to love and befriend them, even as they are beginning to desert us.

Cherish your body is a good guide at any age. People who have lived through serious illness or near-death experiences learn it. They come back to health with a greater appreciation, wanting to use what they have as a vehicle of life. Elderhood, an approaching-death experience, brings this appreciation slowly and gracefully.

Successful elders have a well-seasoned, earthy, realistic physicality. They accept their bodies as they are, without pretense or unrealistic demands, and with respect and tolerance. Our bodies are like dear old friends who have served us well. The fact that they are threatening to leave makes us appreciate them even more.

. . . .

How do you appreciate and cherish your body?

Guide 2: *Stretch and Learn*

The second guide for managing decline is: *Keep stretching.*

Humans are active animals. Our bodies and minds are meant to be used, and respond to use by building competence and power. They respond to disuse by losing some of that competence and power. We have a tendency to contract and shrink, and we must keep stretching to counteract this tendency and keep growing. What we do not use, we lose, not because of our age but because of our passivity. Growth and learning are the flip side of decline. They are our stretching, expansive energies which are continuously counteracting the pervasive, perennial drag of entropy.

The best stretching aims not merely to maintain the condition we have achieved, but to grow. We grow by stretching beyond our current limits and learning new knowledge, skills and habits. Another version of this guide is: *Keep learning.*

We need to stretch our whole organism and all of our functions, especially our minds. Some uninspired oldsters stop reading, give up stimulating conversation, and stop challenging their minds. Like any other organ, a brain that is not stretched shrinks.

The main organ that we must keep stretching is the brain.

It is a great tragedy to look upon "retirement" and old age primarily as a time of inactivity—a time when we no longer need to be active, to think, to stretch ourselves. To adopt such an attitude is to begin to die. Successful elders do not buy it.

Elders do not need to keep racing like youths or plodding like midlifers. We develop our own, gentler ways of stretching.

Use it or lose it.

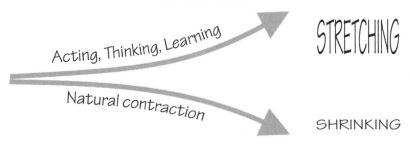

What is shrinking in your life? How are you stretching? What are you learning? Are you stretching your mind?

Guide 3: *Let Go*

The third guide is: *Let go of what no longer fits for you or is no longer available.*

This guide is a stumbling block for many. We are trained in getting and in holding on; we are not trained in letting go. Through midlife we are busy accumulating things. The more we have, the more successful we feel. In later life there is a profound shift in values as we realize that the wealth we have and the things we have accumulated are transitory. We cannot take them with us. Extravagant possessions are tempting paramours in midlife; they become perfidious harlots in age. We still need money and some of the treasures of midlife as resources, but these things are no longer at the center of life. We search for something better and more enduring.

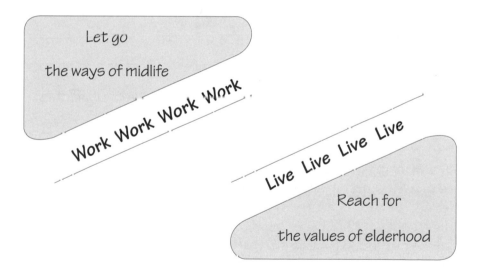

Have you been trained to hold on? Have you learned how to let go? How could you learn now?

The Losses of Elderhood

Elderhood is full of losses; there is much to let go of. Some things, like the drudgery of midlife work, we turn away from willingly, and good riddance. Others, like the physical agility of youth, we lose slowly and begrudgingly. Still others, like the death of a mate, are a sudden and severe blow.

Some losses are inevitable; others are not. The greatest loss of all is avoidable: it is the loss of dreams and expectations by those who think that life is over, and surrender prematurely. That is the tragedy of elderhood unlived.

In any loss, part of our accustomed life disappears, leaving us empty and bereft. If the loss is irretrievable, there is no effective choice but to let go. Holding on to outworn habit is an attempt to cling to a part of life that is already gone, and that no longer serves. Yet we have been closely attached to the lost thing. It has been an important parts of our life, and we need to grieve the loss of that which was close to our heart.

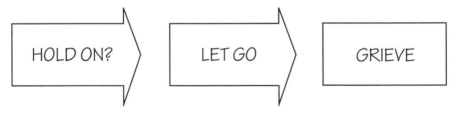

Recurring loss is a familiar pattern in elderhood, and the need to grieve comes up again and again. Even if we are not trained to let go, we cannot escape the need. If we have not developed skill in letting go earlier, we need to develop it in elderhood. If we have not learned how to grieve deeply and effectively, we need to learn in elderhood. Letting go and grieving loss are needed again and again, and successful elders learn how to do both well.

Letting go and grieving are skills of elderhood.

If you survive, you lose friends.

There is an unexpected payoff for grieving. Every grieved loss prepares the way to a new gain, attachment, or goal.

Are you skilled at grieving? Can you do it well, when you must? If not, can you learn how?

Guide 4: *Adapt*

The fourth guide is: *Adapt to new life situations.* Adaptation is the most important single mechanism for productive living in the older years.

There is a myth that elders cannot change: "You can't teach an old dog new tricks." It is deadly to accept this myth and to invite rigidity. It can happen at any age, for rigidity is hardly exclusive to the old.

The myth is partly true, for elders are somewhat more exposed to neural and physiological dysfunction. There is increasing danger of disease, but degenerative disease is the exception, not the rule. Most rigidity is due to our expectations, not the condition of our brains. Older people are *expected* to behave in rigid ways, and those who have not developed the personal strength and independence to resist this expectation may docilely do what is expected of them. Such behavior is more appropriate to youth than to age.

The expectation of rigidity is also based on the assumption that life is over. But it is not over, and as long as life goes on in this changing world, there will be the need to keep on adapting. Successful elders have already become good at it, for they have been adapting all their lives.

. . . .

How rigid, or how adaptable, do you plan to be as you age?
How will you implement your plan?

Accepting Physical Loss

In the context of loss, a good general strategy is to keep compensating for what is lost by adding something new. Aging inevitably brings loss, but it also brings increased experience, learning, and perhaps wisdom. Any loss will leave us with a hole, and we may feel empty. But emptiness is a space with capacity to be filled, and there is always something available to fill it.

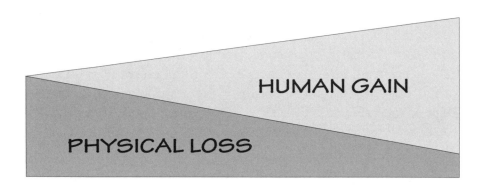

Most physical losses are gradual, and are accompanied by gradual, concurrent maturing. As the body slows down, the human supplement more than compensates for the physical decline. The slowdown of the body is so gradual that we can compensate naturally and smoothly. Our physical vision may be less precise, but because we have seen so much, our effective vision is vaster. Our hearing may become less acute, yet we hear more. A youth of 20 listening to Tchaikowski's *Capriccio Italian* may primarily hear sound, or even noise. An elder of 70, listening to it at lower volume, will hear more music and is more likely to understand and appreciate what Tchaikowski is saying.

Physical perception declines, but human perception increases.
. . . .
How have you compensated for gradual or sudden loss in your life? Did you find something new to fill the empty space?

Elder Energy Budget.

Moving into elderhood usually calls for some downscaling. As our energy fades, we can no longer spend it as recklessly as we did in youth, or as persistently as we did in midlife. We need to spend more time in maintenance, and in recharging our batteries. Earlier in life we may have kept on going even though our batteries were run down and almost dead. Our bodies somehow took the abuse and kept on going. In elderhood we cannot abuse our bodies so and get away with it, nor do we want to.

Most elders have much they want to do, so they are interested in using their limited energy efficiently and to best advantage. They have an energy budget, and must operate within it.

The energy of elderhood is actually very elastic. We want to spend it on things that are truly important. That is the secret of the efficiency of elder energy.

. . . .

In your aging, have you wanted to do the same things with less energy? Or have you wanted to select what you do more carefully because of limited energy?

Chapter 15

The Growth of Spirit

In our view, elderhood involves the development of the person beyond body and beyond ego. In that land of Beyond dwells spirit, waiting to be discovered and pursued.

Topics:

Weakening Body, Growing Spirit

Death and Spirituality

The Quality of Spirit

The Challenge of Spirit

Mature Religion

The Search for Immortality

Weakening Body, Growing Spirit

A central fact of life as we know it is that we are incarnate—we are tied to our bodies. In youth this is so obvious that we hardly notice it, for our partnership with our bodies is very close. With age, however, as our bodies weaken, we can no longer depend on them as much, and are less willing to equate body with self. This life partner in whom we have put our trust is beginning to let us down. We cannot rely on it as we could in the past, and we know that in the end it is going to betray us.

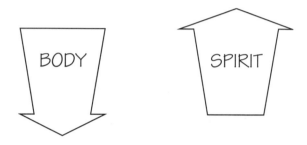

Then we feel the need to search beyond our bodies, looking for something more dependable, more lasting, more essential. We find our spirits.

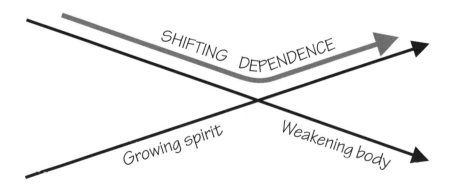

If we are fortunate enough to make a good connection with spirit, it supports us like a skyhook. As spirit grows and becomes more robust, our identification with our bodies decreases.

. . . .

How has your connection with your spirit changed throughout life? Is your spirit growing with age?

Death and Spirituality

The acceptance of death is the door to spirituality. It invites and demands a shift from a material orientation to one that reaches beyond matter, for matter is failing. In the broadest sense, this means that we move from reliance on ego to acceptance of something greater, of which we are part. We move from the realism of Popeye's philosophy—"I am what I am"—to the spiritual awareness that "I am more than I seem to be. There is something beyond me, and I participate in it." Spirituality is the skyhook by which we transcend our bodies and the oblivion they face. It is the window through which we glimpse our cosmic home.

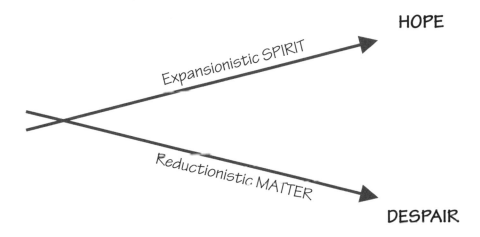

Our culture has been in love with matter, seduced by our competence in dealing with it. As a result we neglected spirit, and even denied it. As we age, we need to find and reclaim spirit.

. . . .

How would you describe your spirituality?

The Quality of Spirit

Spirituality is the way we humans reach beyond ourselves. Virtually everybody experiences and practices some form of spirituality, for everybody feels some connectedness to more than what he or she is. Through spirit we connect beyond time, space, and personality.

The spirituality of age operates in a different dimension from the materialistic dimension of youth and the economic dimension of midlife. It is expansionistic rather than reductionistic. It includes rather than excludes. It seeks to appreciate rather than explain, to love rather than analyze. It does not bring everything within currently measured bounds in a scientific way. Rather, it seeks to reach outside current limits. It is more interested in trusting than in explaining, in embracing than in judging.

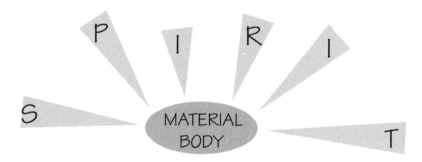

Spirit stretches to the world beyond our time and space—a shadowy world shared by everyone. It reaches beyond that which we can grasp, understand, and control. It reaches beyond what can be neatly explained. It deals with reaching rather than grasping. It implies the willingness to reach even when we know that what we reach for is beyond our grasp.

Spirit does not necessarily embrace a particular God concept or religious belief system, but it always reaches beyond the ego to a trust in a greater basis for our lives.

Spirit follows the *Stretch* guide; reaching beyond ourselves is the ultimate stretching. The *Use it or lose it* rule also applies: if we do not reach beyond ourselves, we shrink within ourselves.

. . . .

What is your spiritual belief, and how does it motivate your life?

The Challenge of Spirit

Our spirit becomes more robust as our body becomes more frail. The shift to spirit reshuffles all our values.

The physical mission of elderhood is to manage the decline of dwindling physical energy. The spiritual mission is to live with and manage our swelling spiritual energy. This is not to deny death but to affirm the fullness of *old*.

In elderhood we need some form of religious engineering, one that cherishes and optimizes spirit rather than busyness. Efficiency has a new meaning. We shift from midlife's efficiency of producing to elderhood's efficiency of being.

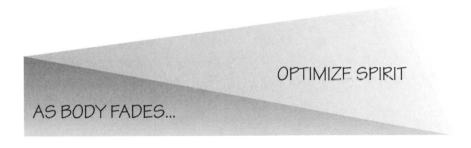

OPTIMIZE SPIRIT

AS BODY FADES...

There are two enemies that tend to strangle spirit. The first is reductionistic thinking, which holds that what is ungraspable does not exist. The second is overwrought religion that goes beyond reaching into grasping, and that holds dogmatically that the Ungraspable has been grasped, and the Ineffable defined.

If we settle for what we can bring comfortably within our grasp, we settle for too narrow a universe. If we pretend we have grasped what we reach for, even when it is in fact beyond our grasp, we trivialize our universe in an attempt to grasp it. When we grasp something too firmly, we squeeze spirit from it. Spirit deals with the beyond. Beyondness is its essence. All we can do is trust and live, day by day.

If you are willing to reach beyond what you can grasp, what will you do with the rest of your life?

Mature Religion

Elders need a relationship with that force that is beyond them, commonly called God. But the relationship of humans to a surpassing divinity is elusive and fuzzy. God speaks in a muffled voice. Listeners hear different messages. It is the nature of humankind that we cannot define God. We cannot avoid reaching for God, but cannot grasp that elusive essence. We sense it chiefly through our own essence. We reach for Beyond from within.

Elders are reachers into the beyond.

For many, belonging to a church is a good channel toward spirituality, but it is not the only channel. Successful elders join a church if it helps them with their religious engineering; otherwise, they find a different avenue to spirit that works for them.

We elders are, in a sense, our own theologians; we are interpreters of the divine in this life. We stand on the edge of life, from where we can reach into the beyond. We must accept responsibility for building our own mature spirituality.

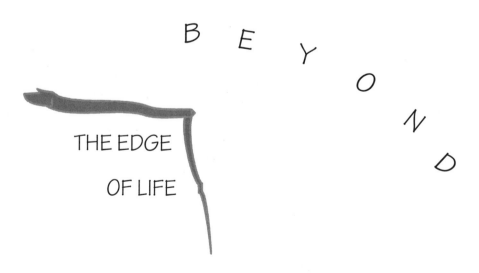

Does your experience in spirituality and religion lead you to agree or disagree?

The Search for Immortality

We all yearn for an abiding presence and undying influence in this world. Seeking some form of continuity beyond death, serious elders ask two questions:

Will the world be any better because I have lived here?
What will remain of me in this world after my death?

Here are some common ways that people seek immortality:

♦ *Progeny*. Many achieve genetic continuity and live on through children and grandchildren, who are reared with the implicit hope that they will in some ways surpass their parents.

♦ *Dissemination of influence.* There is a kind of genetics of spirit. The quality of our spirit rubs off on others who are attuned to us, and they continue to express it in their own way. This influence is not limited by blood lines; we can spread our spirit among any who are willing to absorb it. Human teachers, great and small, live on in this way.

♦ *Personal works and monuments*. Some make works of art, build organizations, or erect buildings or monuments that will outlive them and carry on their name.

♦ *Charities*. Others, having accumulated money, are satisfied to leave a bequest to support causes or projects they favor. Thus they hope to leave the world better in some small way as a result of their having lived here for a while.

♦ *Afterlife*. Many believe that our spirits survive our bodies and life goes on in some way after death—resurrection, karma, reincarnation, heaven, and other religious beliefs.

Regardless of how we seek immortality, our task in elderhood is to finish *this* life as well as we can.

Progeny   Influence   Works   Charities   Afterlife

How do you view immortality?

Chapter 16
The Closing Years

In nature, death follows full maturity. It calls for preparation, readiness, and closure. After we have achieved fullness and are ready, death seems more natural and acceptable.

Topics:

Being Ready

A Finite View of Life

Planning Your Death

Planning From Death to Life

Unfinished Business

Closure

Dying and Death

A Time for Dying

Creative Dying

Being Ready

There are three stages of readiness for death:

♦ *Preparatory readiness.* This is the business part of readiness, such as legal, financial, and property arrangements. It is the cleaning up of the detritus of life, and the passing on of what has value. We can achieve preparatory readiness at any time. It is best to do so early, then keep up to date as we age.

♦ *Readiness through wholeness.* Elders ask, "Will I be ready to die well when my time comes? Will I have lived a full life? Will I have realized the essence of who I am?" Much of the fear of dying is the unwillingness to let go of life unlived. Death after a life not fully lived, regardless of age, seems somehow premature, like the death of a child. Death after a fully lived life seems more fitting and natural, like winter after autumn. A good elderhood strategy, therefore, is to live more fully, then die more willingly. Achieving readiness through wholeness is the major work of elderhood, and usually takes many years.

♦ *Final readiness.* Final readiness is saying good-bye. It is the business of bringing final closure to life as death comes close.

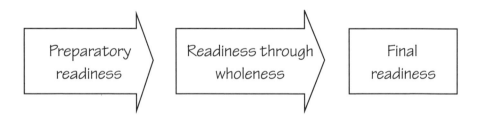

. . . .

Have you taken care of preparatory readiness? How? Are you working on readiness through wholeness? How?

A Finite View of Life

We elders learn to deal with our limits. We see an end to life, and a limited time to reach completion.

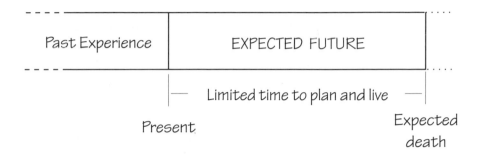

This is the life view of elderhood. It is profoundly different from the life view of youth, which assumes that life goes on indefinitely. So youth plans by extending experience, as if the experiment of life can go on forever. Elders, seeing a more limited future, seek to bring life to completion.

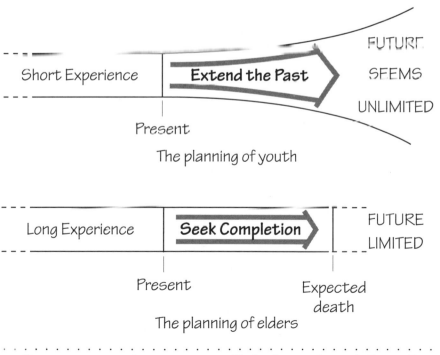

Do you see your future as an unlimited experiment? Or as limited and requiring completion? Or part of both?

Planning Your Death

Since death is inevitable, at what age do you want to go about it? What quality of life do you want in the meantime? What do you want the process of dying to be like?

You can plan your death, and you do so when you make such comments as "I don't want to live as a vegetable" or "Most of my ancestors lived long lives." The statement, "My father died at 68," raises the question whether one intends to die at the same age, sooner, or to live longer than the age suggested by his example. Even the decision not to think about or plan for death at all implies that your plan is to be surprised by it when it comes.

Of course, we do not have full control over the timing and conditions of our death, but we have some control, and our intention may have a significant influence on how things turn out. If our intention is to live, we invite and mobilize energy, and we are more likely to act in ways that maintain our health. If our intention is to die, life energy begins to seep out and desert us.

Here is an example of a reasonable death plan:

I want to live as long as I can maintain human vitality, alertness, and joy. I want to bring my life to closure and die consciously, with as little pain as possible.

At this time I plan to die at about age 93, at home, after a brief illness, with time to say good-bye to family and close friends.

You can modify your plan at any time. If you are unable to maintain the level of health you want, you may lower your age of expected death. If, on the other hand, you have chosen age 87 and are still full of joy and energy at 86, revise the age upward.

· ·

What is your conscious plan?

Planning from Death to Life

Foreseeing your death helps you to plan the remainder of your life. A successful elder makes life plans with a realistic view of limited time. The pursuit of completion adds focus and realism, and generates more human vitality. Life is not seen as an unlimited and uncharted expansion, but as a process with limited scope and with integrity.

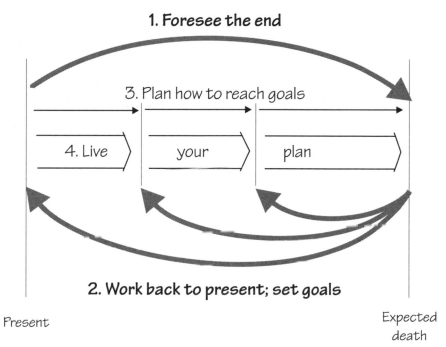

Working back from death, you can take the measure of life. You can ask: How much time do I have? What do I want to become before I die? What are my intermediate goals? What do I need to do to achieve them?

Working backwards from your death is a good way to plan ahead.

. . . .

In view of a limited life, what are your intermediate goals? What is your schedule?

Unfinished Business

Elders ask, "What unfinished business is there in my life?"

The question is appropriate at any age, for death is not restricted to elders. It can come, unsuspected, at any time. We do not know when we will die, but in elderhood we know it is getting closer, and we want to be ready. We do not want to leave behind much unfinished business. This does not mean that we stop doing things; healthy elders tend to have active and productive projects as along as we live. It means we take care of what we reasonably can to achieve a good level of readiness.

We finish up some business for the benefit of those who survive us, and from their viewpoint. By making wills or trusts, for example, we ease the transition from society-with-living-us to society-without-living-us. We arrange to use our resources as long as we need them, then pass them on (with minimal taxes) or put them to the work we choose. We may arrange for the disposal of our body, either to get the treatment we want for it, or to save our family from having that task at the stressful time of our death.

PERSONAL EFFECTS

BEQUESTS

RELATIONSHIPS

Mostly, we will want to finish any unfinished business from our personal viewpoint, to simplify life and remove its clutter. In age we tend to put out the trash of life more faithfully, and to neaten up after ourselves. We clean out the closets of life and give away or throw away what no longer serves us. We burn our old journals or personal papers in ritual, or leave instructions for their burning. It is not fair to leave a mess for others to clean.

We keep our relationships tidier. We say what needs to be said, rather than putting it off until some future opportunity, which may not arrive.

In age we clean out the closets of life.

Have you minimized the unfinished business you will leave behind? How?

Closure

Like any good story, life has a beginning, a middle, and an ending stage. In a broad sense, elderhood is the ending stage. We need to do the things suitable for endings, even though we plan to live for decades. It is a time of summary, tying together, bringing to completion, and closure.

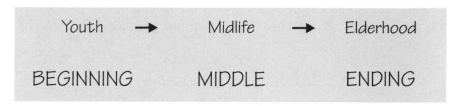

Youth	→	Midlife	→	Elderhood
BEGINNING		MIDDLE		ENDING

To achieve closure is to "round out" an event, to end gracefully and smoothly, without rough edges, and to provide a suitable transition to what follows. In much of life we are swept abruptly from one activity to another without closure. Busy with efficient production, we run life like an assembly line rather than giving each task and each experience the attention and reverence it deserves. That is like living without dancing. It is a pity to go through elderhood like that. Elderhood is a dancing time. Each event is brought to closure, and finally all of life is brought to closure.

Much of earlier life is expansive and accumulative, adding more stuff. Elderhood is integrative and congealing. We work with the stuff we have earlier accumulated and fit it together like a work of art. It is a long, gradual wrapping up, rounding out, completing, and closing.

More than ever we must manipulate our world, but now it is a manipulation of art rather than acquisition.

At the very end, as death calls, we put the final touches on that work of art and say it is done.

. . . .

At this time in life, do you have the inclination and leisure to round out life events and bring them to closure? Do you yet feel the need to bring your whole life to closure? How will you do that?

Dying and Death

Acknowledging death is one thing; dying is another. Dying is a process of physical life; death is the final event in that process. Death is abstract to the living, yet occurs with concrete finality.

In a broad sense, we die little by little; it happens gradually throughout our lives. All the losses of life are little dyings. Finally, dying culminates as the terminal process of this life, the letting go of the body, the surrendering of physical life—death.

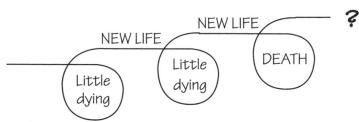

Throughout life and up to the moment of death, both an inclining life force and a declining death force are at work in the body in dynamic tension. The body is both dying and healing, letting go of the old and taking on the new, keeping a dynamic balance. In the final dying process, the life force weakens and the death force gets the upper hand. Finally, the one gives way and the other takes over. Then, on the physical level, decline is shockingly sudden, and the body quickly loses the characteristics of life. What happens on other levels we can only speculate.

Death is a major life experience, equaled only by the experience of birth. Yet we tune it out, because we are afraid of it. The fear is real; it can be reduced but not eliminated. Some of it is the fear of pain; much of it is the fear of the unknown. The adventure we face at death is sketched by faith, and the process is perhaps hinted at by parapsychology, yet we enter it blindly. We are not entirely without experience—we faced a great unknown at birth, and lesser unknowns throughout life. The unknown we face at death is the greatest of all.

We can prepare for this philosophically, then postpone the reality until we must face it.

. . . .

Are you living your dying or waiting for death by thinking about it as little as possible?

A Time for Dying

There comes a time for dying. It may be thrust upon us by accident or disease, or it may creep up with gradual physical decline. Or we may feel that we have brought our life to completion and we are ready to go. For most, there eventually comes a time when it is clear that decline has the upper hand and the final dying process is underway. Our bodies signal that they are in a terminal phase. Despite our maintenance efforts, our bodies give up. Usually, the dying process is relatively short, a small fraction of life, perhaps a few months, perhaps less.

Sometimes the approach of death is clear and inevitable, sometimes it is uncertain. We may need to ask these questions and make judgments:

Are the signs clear that the final process is underway? If I survive, will the conditions of life be acceptable? Am I ready to die, or can I become ready? How much do I want to fight for more life?

At 40 one might fight a cancer with all available resources. At 85 one might not. It is not merely a matter of age. If life feels complete, we may be more willing to close it.

If one is ready to let go, the compulsive competence of modern medicine may become an impediment rather than an asset. Too often, when a dying elder wants to let go with deliberation and dignity, family and friends are not ready or willing to let that happen, or do not know how. Often they do not have the wisdom or courage not to dial 911 or call for extreme measures of holding on. Medicine becomes an obstacle course rather than a savior. Dying becomes medical monstrosity and failure, stripped of dignity.

Alternatively, we may close life as we close each day, in sleep when it is fitting, not staggering on until we fall of exhaustion.

. . . .

Do you expect that a time will come when it is fitting and desirable for you to die? Do you hope to do so gracefully?

Creative Dying

One goal of elderhood is to die well. If death is inevitable, let it be a victory, at least a natural process. The alternative is to approach death as if in a driverless carriage hurtling toward the edge of a cliff.

In the ritual of creative dying, the dying person says, in effect:

I want to celebrate the end of me as I know me in this body, ending as well as I can. I am not a god, so I give up any pretense of physical immortality; it gets in the way of ending. If there is an afterlife I welcome it, but first I want to bring this life to graceful ending. I have sympathy for those who survive me, and who are not ready for ending, as I am. I am facing my limits, and am ready to let go. I want to do so with as much awareness as I can manage.

Creative dying is the final stage of living, a positive relinquishing. It calls for awareness, even though that may be difficult to achieve. As in so much of life, once again at the end we face a trade-off between pain and consciousness. If we manage to achieve consciousness, it may bring the final, intense bloom of maturity, in which we are more lucid, frank, and peaceful than ever before.

After dying comes death. Whatever that is, and whatever it brings, it will inevitably come. And we shall know it in whatever way it is known.

· ·

When your time comes, how can you die well?

Afterword

We find joy—or it finds us—along the everyday trail, in simple and unexpected places. We find it by being ourselves and by making compassionate connection, essence-to-essence, with fellow creatures of any type. When joy possesses us, we resonate in it.

Joy is the resonance of heart and spirit attuned to essence and free to vibrate. In elderhood, when our spirits are strongly emerging, when we dwell with our hearts in the present, have more leisure, and seek essence, we are in a favorable position to know mature joy.

We are open to joy when our hearts and spirits are not stuck in the past or restricted by ageism, especially when they are not damped by our own bias against aging. A modern challenge is to keep our hearts and spirits free to vibrate with the joy of *old*.

So what? Knowing what you have learned in these pages, what will you do as a result? How will you be in elderhood?

The human spirit seems, in mysterious ways, to reach back beyond birth, and forward beyond death. It enfolds us like a loving angel, hugging us tightly to form and enclose this life as we know it. Within this life, we reach our full development in elderhood.

Looking back, life is like a play in which we are both audience and performer, improvising our life plot as we go along. It is a play in three acts, each with its own theme, each different, developing the plot further. We have reached the third act, called Elderhood, in which our play reaches its dramatic climax.

There are no fixed lines to speak; we live our life story and gather substance as we go along. The play rolls on with a persistent rhythm, through stable periods, then transitions, then new stability with a new theme. It does not work well to continue to use the theme of the first act when we are in the second, or to hang on to the theme of the second act when we reach the third.

Our society encourages us through the first and second acts; we enter the third act on our own. Having grown accustomed to the earlier acts, we may be reluctant to move on. Not yet familiar with the theme of the third act, we may feel anxious until we discover that the story grows richer in human drama and humor.

Unaware of this growing richness, society assumes that the first two acts are best, and suggests that the play is over after the second act. But the play of life has a surprise ending as the final and essential theme develops. The third act is the more enjoyable because its joy is unexpected.

No phase of life is inherently better than any other. Every stage of life has its ups and downs, its advantages and disadvantages, its life energy and death energy. *Making the most of what you've got is what matters at any age.*

As our life story rolls on, here are some of the surprises that come in the third act:

You were told you are out to pasture, finished with life. But it turns out you are in one more life transition into another phase, with different possibilities and different handicaps.

You were told growth is finished, that it's all downhill now. It turns out that the most challenging development of life is at hand.

You were told you can no longer change and learn. It turns out you are entering unexplored territory and must be a pioneer and an entrepreneur.

You were told you are fading away. It turns out you are finally in touch with the lightness of being, becoming more fully human than ever before.

You were told you are no longer valuable. It turns out you have just what our culture now needs.

You were told elders are dull. It turns out that successful elders are mature, present, involved, passionate, free, candid, grateful, loving, spiritual, peaceful, humorous, and joyful.

Welcome to the joy of old!

So enjoy!

INDEX

Entries corresponding to headings are given in initial capitals.

Related Books

The Adult Years: Mastering the Art of Self-Renewal, by Frederic M. Hudson. San Francisco, Jossey-Bass, 1991, hardback.

LifeLaunch: A Passionate Guide to the Rest of Your Life, by Frederic M. Hudson and Pamela D. McLean. Santa Barbara, The Hudson Institute Press, 1994, softback.

Related Seminars

Conducted by The Hudson Institute of Santa Barbara

LifeLaunch—The basic course for managing personal and organizational change.

ElderLaunch; Building a Positive Elderhood—This seminar is based on the principles of successful elderhood contained in this book, applied to the practical issues of everyday elder life.

Protire, Don't Retire—For persons facing the twin tasks of redefining life that was work-centered and becoming successful elders.

For more information, see next page or call
The Hudson Institute of Santa Barbara
(800) 582-4401

For more copies or more information
visit your bookstore or . . .

ORDER FORM

[ ] Please send:

_____ copies of *The Joy of Old* at $16.95 each _____

_____ copies of *LifeLaunch* at $16.95 each _____

_____ copies of *The Adult Years* at $26.95 each _____

Sales tax:
For books shipped to a California address,
please add 7.75% or local California rate. _____

Shipping:
$2.00 for the first book,
$1.00 for each additional book. _____

[ ] Check enclosed: Total: _____

[ ] Please send information on related seminars.

Please send the books and information to:

Name: _____

Address: _____

City: _____ State: _____ Zip: _____

Send your order to:

Geode Press
P.O. Box 6077
Altadena, CA 91003-6077

(818) 797-7684